THE CHRIST OF THE
NEW TESTAMENT

THE
CHRIST OF THE
NEW TESTAMENT

BY
PAUL ELMER MORE

GREENWOOD PRESS, PUBLISHERS
NEW YORK

Come, royal Name; and pay the expense
Of all this precious patience;
　　　O come away,
And kill the death of this delay.
O see so many worlds of barren years
Melted and measured out in seas of tears.
O see the weary lids of wakeful hope
(Love's eastern windows) all wide ope
　　　With curtains drawn,
To catch the day-break of thy dawn.

Richard Crashaw

PREFACE

It was originally my intention to cover the whole
range of theology down to the year 451 in a single volume, and to limit my study of the New
Testament to an episode in that treatise. But
the material so grew under my hand, and in particular the impossibility of bringing Christianity into the Greek Tradition without a fuller
consideration of the person and teaching of Jesus
became so apparent, that I have been forced to
divide the projected volume into two, the first of
which is herewith offered to the public. At the
same time, though the book has thus its place in
a lengthening series, I have aimed to make it
complete in itself so that it may be read alone as
an independent work.

After a good deal of hesitation I came to the
decision that it would be best to cut down the
notes to the barest necessity. This procedure is
open to serious objections; it lends an air of nov-
elty and dogmatic assurance which it is far from
my wish to adopt. But on the other side the difficulty of setting a bound to annotation, if once
I took that course, appeared to me insuperable.

Every statement of fact or theory would need
to be buttressed by authorities and defended
against impugners, and the discussion involved
would have swollen the notes to a bulk out of all
proportion to the text. To the indurated scholar
such a treatment might have been welcome, to
most readers it would have been a meaningless
distraction.

In the absence of references I may take this
occasion to acknowledge my special indebted-
ness to Johannes Weiss, Schweitzer, Kabisch,
Wendt, and Eduard Meyer; indeed I might say
that my position in regard to the literary and
historical problems of Biblical criticism represents what seem to me the solid results of the
past century of German investigation. To the
philosophy, however, that has lain behind this
scholarship, tacit or avowed, my attitude is not
at all receptive, but definitely hostile. If in fact
my study of the New Testament has any value,
it will be in this separation of German scholarship from the regnant German philosophy, and
in the endeavour to show how the achievements
of the higher criticism may be accepted without
succumbing to a purely humanitarian view of
Christianity.

In quoting from the Old Testament I have

followed chiefly the Authorized Version and Professor Kent's translation. My Hebrew is not sufficient to warrant an independent judgement in obscure passages, but I trust that my interpretations will be found faithful to the spirit of the original.

P. E. M.

Princeton, New Jersey
January 2, 1924

CONTENTS

THE CHRIST OF THE
NEW TESTAMENT

CHAPTER I

OTHERWORLDLINESS AND MORALITY

IT is well when we start out on a long journey to know the port for which we are bound, and the reader who is preparing to go with me on this venture of criticism may like to hear in advance the conclusion we are to reach. Fortunately for reader and writer, that conclusion is clear, and can be stated in few words: it is simply the so-called Definition pronounced by the fourth ecumenical Council at Chalcedon, in A.D. 451, which reaffirms, in sharper and more positive terms, the central thesis of the Faith as it was formulated by the first ecumenical Council at Nicea in the year 325. One thing the Church declared to be obligatory, one belief henceforth should distinguish the Christian from all other men: Christ was a person who embraced within himself the full nature of divinity and the full nature of humanity.[1] This too, and really nothing more, is the subject of the present volume and its sequel. Our purpose, I need to say with emphasis, is not to prove exactly the truth of this thesis of the Incarnation —for such proof would require a line of argument, historical and apologetic, which lies outside of our course—but to show that the Incarnation, so understood, is, as it claims to be, the one essential dogma of Christianity, that the philosophy underlying it conforms to our deepest spiritual experience, that it is the mythological expression (using the word "mythological" in no derogatory sense) of the Platonic dualism, and thus forms a proper consummation of the Greek Tradition.

Such is the goal of our journey, clearly defined certainly, whether repellent or attractive. But it cannot be said that the way thereto presents no difficulties. On the contrary, it is well to be forewarned that the whole bent of higher

[1] The exact language of the Faith as pronounced at Nicea and defined at Chalcedon may be left to the volume in which we shall deal with the history of Greek theology. It is sufficient here to say that the clear purpose of the Definition of Chalcedon was to express in technical terms the statement made above. The Faith of Nicea, of which the Definition is a confirmation and expansion, must not be confused with the Creed, "commonly called the Nicene," which embraces many things not mentioned in the authoritative statement of dogma pronounced by the first and fourth Councils.

criticism during the last hundred years has been directed against this Definition of Chalcedon, or, to speak more precisely, has proceeded on the assumption that the union of two natures in one person offers an incredible paradox. Thus, at the outset of his masterly account of the Christology of the past century, Schweitzer says:

"First of all it was necessary to shatter this dogma before the historic Jesus could be resought, before indeed any idea of his existence could be entertained. That he is something other than the Jesus Christ of the two-nature doctrine, seems to us now a self-evident commonplace. It is hard for us at this day even to comprehend the long agony of thought in which our historical view of Jesus was born. When he came to be reawakened into life, he still wore the bandages of death, as did Lazarus—the bandages of the two-nature dogma."[2]

This is the prologue to the best survey of the range of German criticism, confirmed by every page of the ensuing history. And its repercussion, though delayed, has been heard among the more cautious theologians of England. To the chaplain, for instance, of the Archbishop of Canterbury, a scholarly churchman in good standing, "the formula of Chalcedon is, in fact, a

[2] *Geschichte der Leben-Jesu-Forschung,* 3.

confession of the bankruptcy of Greek Patris-
tic theology";[3] and the writer of a popular treatise on the Gospel of John, referring to this same
formula, declares that "in the later theology the
speculative theory of the person of Christ was
carried out to its logical issue, and resulted in
endless confusion, and in the substitution of a
barren dogma for a divine faith."[4] Against such
formidable opposition we have to maintain that
dogma is not barren, that the theology of the Fathers is in no wise bankrupt, and that nothing in
modern thought—the very word "modern" implies a begging of the question, for thought is
the same yesterday and today—has shaken the
philosophic truth which lies behind the Definition.

To begin with we should get clear in our minds
that the assumption of modern criticism not only
undermines the foundation of Christianity but
strikes at the root of all religion whatsoever. Oh,
I know how the chaplain of Lambeth and the
seven wise men of Oxford would cry out against
such an imputation, how indignantly they would
protest they were only pouring the old wine into
new bottles; I know how from Schleiermacher

[3] William Temple, in *Foundations, a Statement of Christian Belief in Terms of Modern Thought, by Seven Oxford Men*, 230.
[4] Ernest F. Scott, *The Fourth Gospel*, 162.

to Harnack the long line of theologians over the water have boasted that they were merely purging religion of its dross, lifting it from the low level of Greek intelligence to the purer altitudes of Teutonic spirituality; and I do not doubt their sincerity. Yet somehow, as one plods through the literature, one cannot escape the feeling that in this reverent decantation and this Germanization not Christianity alone has been spilled or left behind, but the very essential matter that gives substance to faith. For what is religion? To answer that question some patience is required and not a little humility.

Now religion, as I take it, is the union of otherworldliness—the term is not satisfactory, but I know no better—of otherworldliness, then, and morality; and these two elements are dependent on the mysterious duality of mind and Ideas and on the equally mysterious duality of good and evil. This is the twin paradox which rationalism is always busy in explaining away, careless of the fact that in so doing it invariably falls into still more perplexing contradictions of its own creation. It is odd, but true, that reasonableness and rationalism have never been able to dwell together peaceably; hence the need of humility.

The best approach to the dualism of mind and Ideas lies through the analogous paradox which confronts us in every act of our daily life, and which the plain man accepts with no more ado. I mean the obvious fact that we live in a double world of mental and material phenomena, that somehow we are both mind and body. This conjunction of mind and body is so familiar a part of our experience that we are apt to forget its strangeness, though in truth nothing in religion is more irrational or more incomprehensible. Indeed, it may be questioned whether one who has honestly faced this mystery, with all its implications, will find any serious intellectual difficulty in the postulates of religion. The point is that we have no means of expressing our knowledge except in those terms of space and quantity which pertain to body and material phenomena, whereas the knowing mind cannot be defined in either of these terms. There stands this body of mine, which I see extended in space, through which various sensations reach me, and with which my life is so intimately associated. I seem to know it and to be able to define it—though in the end my seeming ability here too may turn out an illusion; but what is this per-

ceiving mind, in what corresponding terms shall
I define this consciousness which I know as myself? Certainly, my feeling itself of pleasure or
pain, the thoughts in my mind as I write these
words, that which says "my," may indeed be connected with things of space, but they themselves
are not spatial. Where are they? I say they are
in my brain, but, strictly speaking, the very word
"where" has no meaning when applied to them.
Stop and imagine if you can how a thing can
exist, and yet not exist in space.

It is fair to say that philosophy has its beginning in the wonder raised by this puzzling association and interaction of the spatial and non-
spatial. But if that wonder opens the way to
reflection, it may be said also that metaphysics
commonly ends by denying the paradox out of
which philosophy grew. On the one side philosophy had its exit in Berkeley's endeavour to
refine all things away to mind and its ideas, to
which endeavour the proper answer is Dr.
Johnson's contemptuous kicking of a stone in
his path. When the so-called idealist has ceased
to argue, I still know that my world is filled with
brute facts which cannot be reduced to mental
operations. On the other side rise the host of

modern psychologists who are undertaking to define mind in terms of body. The results of their efforts are excruciatingly funny; yet, oddly enough, you will scarcely here and there catch more than a whispered laugh in our halls of learning. *Audi alteram partem.* Let me quote a very modern attempt to express consciousness in terms of potential (mechanical) energy in such a way as to escape the exasperating dualism of mind and body. But first it should be stated that the author is not a humorist but a highly respected professor of philosophy, and that "synapses" are the connecting places of the neurons, or discontinuous particles, which are strung together to form a nerve. Hear now the other side:

"When a vibration-wave proceeding over a sensory nerve is gradually brought to a stop by the resistance of the synapse, its energy is transformed from a visible and kinetic form to an invisible and potential form. As its velocity passes through the zero-phase, its slowness passes through an infinity-phase. I ask you to entertain the suggestion that this *infinity-phase of slowness* is the common stuff of all sensations and that the critical points of zero and infinity through which the motion and the slowness respectively pass, afford the basis for that qualitative absoluteness and discontinuity that differentiate sensations from mere rates of change."[5]

It used to be believed that by the utterance of some cabalistic word like *Abraxas* or *Abracadabra* the demons hostile to man's peace could be laid under a ban. I defy anyone to find among all the magical papyri of Egypt a more naïve trust in the powers of language than this suggestion that the intrusive ghost of consciousness can be exorcized out of the good clean world of mechanics by pronouncing *this-infinity-phase-of-slowness*.[6] But enough.

Now these psychological materialists (of whom there are as many sects and gradations as once divided the heretical Arians) and the Berkeleyans cannot both be right, and it is reasonable to surmise that they are both wrong. Their age-long quarrel would seem to point to the truth, so humiliating to man's pride of intelligence, that our life is a composite of two disparate entities, mind and matter, whose mode of interaction has quite

[5] W. P. Montague, in *Proceedings of the Aristotelian Society* for 1920, Vol. XXI, p. 42. I was directed to this quotation by J. B. Pratt's little book on *Matter and Spirit*. Mr. Pratt, though himself an accredited professor of philosophy, has had the temerity to turn the ineptitudes of modern psychology into a delightful farce. A dualist, indeed, might be defined as a philosopher with a sense of humour.

[6] One is reminded of Epiphanius' comment after citing a long list of cabalistic names employed by the Gnostics: "Such is the fecundity of their illusory imagination, whereby they bring to birth a strange language of empty sounds fit for the invention of any myth" (*Adv. Haer.* xxxi, 4).

eluded, and apparently will forever elude, our research. And if this be so, there follows a further question: how shall we distinguish here between true and false? how shall we even admit any such distinction? If the mind exists by its own right, then the thoughts of the mind have somehow an existence independent of the material world. There they are, all with equal claims to reality; we have them; which are true and which false? in what way does the word false possess any meaning? In ancient times the Cynic Antisthenes had a simple answer to this question, which he put in the form of a syllogism: "Whatever we say [that is, whatever thought exists in the mind] is true: for if we say, we say something; and if we say something, we say that which is; and if we say that which is, we say truth." Argal, it is nonsense to call any idea false. That may sound like a hoary old fallacy, but in fact it is still doing active service in various schools of philosophy; we are still rather fond of asserting that there is no disputing about tastes and opinions, and that what appears true to me *is* true to me, and there's an end on it. A good deal of the energy of Plato's later years was directed to this central stronghold of sophistry, which raises a flag of defiance against all serious philosophy and all religion; and I see no better solution of the difficulty than his pragmatic test in the *Theaetetus* and the *Sophist*.

Suppose I form the notion of a chair in my mind; suppose it suits my fancy to conceive of a two-legged chair. The Cynic would say: there the notion is, like any other concept in my mind; it is something, and so far it is true. But suppose now that I manufacture such a chair, and then sit in it; the result proves pretty quickly that my concept was faulty. The notion of such a chair was false because it was incoherent, or inconsistent with itself; for the conception of a chair means something I can sit in, and I discover by an easy pragmatic test that I cannot sit in a two-legged chair. And, further, my conception of such a chair was impracticable because it comes into conflict with certain physical laws. That is to say, the pragmatic test implies the correspondence of my notions, if they are true, with a physical law over which I have no control, and which has the power of penalizing any infraction of its sway; while the fact that I can conceive false notions shows that the law inherent in the physical world and the activity of my mind are in some respect independent one of the other.

That conclusion would appear to be self-evi-

dent in the spatial mechanical realm which is the
field of science. But there is a whole range of
concepts where the matter is by no means so
simple; and a good deal of confusion has come
about owing to the fact that Plato, who fathered
the theory of Ideas, never quite clearly, or definitely, distinguished between generalizations
which belong to the realm of physics and generalizations which belong to an utterly different
realm. He would argue about the Idea of a table
as if it were the same sort of thing as the Idea of
justice, whereas the former is not properly an
Idea at all.

The difference lies in this, that justice and the
other virtues are not concerned primarily with
brute objects in space and commensurable in
terms of quantity, but with conduct. These conceptions are, however, similar to physical conceptions in this important respect, that our test of
their truth or falsehood is again pragmatic. Take,
for instance, the virtue of justice. A city may
pass certain laws regulating the mutual conduct of men in the matter of property and con-
tract. It will conceive these laws to be just; and
in one sense they are just, so long as they are so
held. But in practice they may effect what this
same city in no wise contemplated, since in the

very word justice we include the expectation of
a beneficial result. The conception of justice
therefore, as applied in detrimental laws, was
false in so far as it was inconsistent with itself;
injustice might thus be defined as an incoherent
conception of justice. And something more than
that comes out in the contrast between present
expectation and future realization: the conception of justice was incoherent because in operation it proved to run counter to a moral force
over which the city had no control, and which
works on in silent irresistible majesty, heedless
of our thinking or our will:

> The unwritten statutes, ever fixed on high,
> Which none of mortal heritage can defy;
> For not of yesterday but to all years
> Their birth, and no man knoweth whence or why.[7]

Now these unwritten laws, of which the de-
crees of a State or the private code of an individual are imperfect copies, constitute what Plato
called Ideas, and we learn by the test of experience that they are objective in the sense that they
are not of man's making or choosing, but have
some sort of incomprehensible existence apart
from our mind. We do indeed speak, Plato himself did so speak, of our moral conceptions as

[7] *Antigone,* 454 et seqq.

Ideas *in* the mind; but this subjective use of the word does not contradict, and must not be permitted to obscure, the fact of a spiritual dualism of the mind and objective Ideas corresponding after a fashion to the physical dualism of mind and material objects. This spiritual dualism is what we mean by the term otherworldliness.

And closely upon the heels of otherworldliness comes the distinction of good and evil as concerned with our motives and states of feeling and innate sense of responsibility. It is not only that we have true or erroneous conceptions of, let us say, justice, but we are conscious also of a certain warfare in our nature, on the one hand of something within us that craves obedience to our conception of justice, and on the other hand of some tendency, some indolence of disposition or lethargy of will, that drags us down to neglect or transgression of what we believe to be right. Here again, in this contrast of good and evil tendencies within our disposition pointing to a like opposition of powers within the universe, we are confronted by a paradox distasteful to reason, and there is a constant temptation to avoid the dilemma by absorbing one member of the dualism in the other. Almost always in practice this rebellion of the *intellectus sibi per-*

missus takes the course of so defining evil as to
make it appear not essentially contrary to good.
That is natural. We seem to understand good,
or at least to believe in it instinctively, since the
good is simply that of which we approve; and
why should there be anything of which we do not
approve, which, so far as we can see, answers to
no approbation anywhere? Hence the constant
pull in philosophy, as displayed notably in the
Stoic and Neoplatonic schools, to slur over evil
by some theory of monism. No doubt it might
be pleaded, as a kind of moral justification of
such theories, that by eliminating the reality of
evil they leave the good in its perfect purity; but
in effect their influence is to weaken the very
sinews of morality and to reduce the soul to a
state of ethical indifference. To one who prizes
the sense of moral responsibility above the claims
of reason the only honest position is to face the
fact of good and evil as an irrational finality; such
an one will reject with indignation any argument
that would flatter away his remorse for base desires and ignoble thoughts and mean actions.

Here, then, in the mysterious dualism of otherworldliness and the equally mysterious dualism
of morality, lies the beginning of religion. Reduced to its lowest terms the religious sense might

be defined, in the language of Matthew Arnold, as the acknowledgement of *a power not ourselves that makes for righteousness*. That is a great phrase, which comes close to the heart of the matter; but I am not so sure that Arnold was progressing quite soundly when, in the same treatise,[8] he went on to find the higher meaning of religion in *morality touched by emotion*. Certainly morality without emotion is a dead thing, but in this supposed development we seem to be in danger of slipping into an irresponsible sentimentalism. I am inclined to think that the truer heightening of religion comes rather—or shall we say primarily?—with Plato's insistence on the imagination as the faculty which lends reality to the factor of otherworldliness in the compound. I should hold that the next and inevitable step in religion, after the bare acknowledgement of *the not ourselves which makes for righteousness,* carries the mind to Plato's symbolical visualization of the world of Ideas as shining and very real entities, existing somehow, to the imagination *somewhere,* out of space and above the sphere of phenomena visible to the eye of flesh. Only so, it seems, can otherworldliness and morality become vividly present to the mind, and

---

[8] *Literature and Dogma.*

only so will religion awaken the soul to strive diligently towards the attainment of its inalienable birthright of peace and glory.

That, I take it, is the heart, the inmost shrine, of religion,—that union of otherworldliness and morality which received its typical expression in the Ideal philosophy of Plato. Without that, so far as I can see, there can be no genuine spiritual experience, with it the doors of the inner life are thrown open, though the mind refuse to take any further step in the mystery of faith. But as a matter of fact religion has never stopped at this point. Always, from the first instinctive sense of otherworldliness to the last most refined preaching of hope, the otherworld of moral Ideas has been peopled with spiritual beings and unbodied personalities of one kind or another. This is what I meant by that extension of the philosophy of religion into theology and mythology which formed the thesis of my *Religion of Plato;* and to that volume I would refer the reader for the arguments in favour of accepting religion in its larger scope. For the present I would offer only this suggestion. If, as seems demonstrable, the otherworld of Ideas does exist somehow apart from the sphere of spatial phenomena, then I can see no philosophical objection to a belief in the existence of unbodied minds in—the word implies locality and space, yet let us say *in* that otherworld. One may grant that the nature of life dissociated from spatial phenomena is indescribable and incomprehensible; but then so is the existence of Ideas incomprehensible, so, equally, is the reality of the material world which lies behind our physical sensations and perceptions. The man who is frightened by the impenetrable wall of mystery that everywhere surrounds us, had better cease to think at all; for faith is inseparable from scepticism. I do not say that the removal of philosophical objections carries with it a positive demonstration of the existence of spiritual beings —by no means. But it does render assent to such a belief possible and even probable; theology and mythology, with their conviction of God and the immortality of the soul, become highly reasonable at the lowest count. It was in this vein that Huxley made his confession:

"I have no *a priori* objections to the doctrine. No man who has to deal daily and hourly with nature can trouble himself about *a priori* difficulties. Give me such evidence as would justify me in believing anything else, and I will believe that. Why should I not? It is not half so won-

derful as the conservation of force, or the in-
destructibility of matter."[9]

Our discussion of religion has proceeded on
the ground that otherworldliness and morality
are inseparable, as ultimately and essentially
they no doubt are. But in actual life the two may
be, or may seem to be, disjoined; at least the emphasis may be placed so strongly on one of the
two that the other disappears from sight.

Thus history presents the all-too common
spectacle of a vigorous belief in the otherworld,
yet with a low or perverted standard of morals.
The Italian bandit who peoples the air with
spirits, and who prays devoutly to the Virgin
Mary or to a patron saint for success in some
act of villainy, is perfectly sincere in his faith,
while the distinction between good and evil would
seem scarcely to exist for him. We know too that
the ardent worship of the gods has been associated in many times and places with vile de-
bauchery. And even where the devotion of the
community remains pure, it is an indisputable
fact that with individuals a heightened otherworldliness is always in danger of running into
some form of antinomianism. This was the peril,
as we shall see elsewhere, which beset the various

[9] Letter to Kingsley, September 23, 1860.

Gnostic sects, and from which orthodox Christians were never safe. The ancient custom of postponing baptism until the last moment of life too often meant nothing more than a desire to continue in the pleasant indulgences of the flesh, with the assurance that by one magical act of lustration the soul would be cleansed and fitted for the hazards of the otherworld.[10]

These are facts not to be denied, and they may seem to throw rather an ugly light on one of the main sources of religion. They signify generally of course that the form in which other-worldliness manifests itself has lagged behind the growth in moral experience, that the community or individual is superstitious rather than religious. Further investigation will show, I think, that the characteristic note of superstition is an undue stress on the belief in ghostly beings or persons hovering about us in the invisible world along with a failure to grasp the reality of impersonal Ideas.

On the other hand it is equally true that we meet men of a pure, even a lofty, morality, yet with no belief in the otherworld at all,—men of whom Huxley may be taken as a conspicuous

[10] The better theologians of the day were fully aware of this disposition among believers. See, for example, Gregory of Nyssa, *De Baptismo*, 425 (Migne).

type. This fact is notorious, and offers perhaps the strongest argument against the truth, or at least the importance, of otherworldliness and religion. In many cases of the sort it is fair to reply that such morality really derives its sap from a religious root, that, though the man himself may deny the connexion, and indeed be unaware of it, his moral sense is a kind of parasitic growth upon the otherworldliness of the society in which he lives. In other cases moral agnosticism may be traced to a deep mental confusion, such as may be seen in the philosophy of Huxley. Here you find a clear sense of the pragmatic value of ethical conceptions together with a failure to draw the logical conclusion that such a pragmatic test implies the objective reality of moral laws, *i.e.*, Ideas. Thus, Huxley was forced by his moral sense to admit that the ethical law of human conduct runs diametrically counter to the law of physical evolution, yet at the same time asserted that Platonic Idealism had been the prime corrupter of intellectual integrity from the beginning to the present day. I do not see how such a position could be held without a profound inconsistency somewhere at the centre of the man's thinking.

But, however you explain these phenomena,

the fact remains that the severance of other-worldliness and morality, whichever of the two overshadows or eliminates the other, is precarious, when it is not fraught with peril. So Joubert put the question: *Qu'est-ce qui est le plus difforme, ou d'une religion* (*i.e.,* otherworldliness) *sans vertu, ou de vertus sans religion?* Otherworldliness without morality degenerates into superstition or a more or less conscious hypocrisy. Morality without otherworldliness loses its large emotional and imaginative values, and, being deprived of its proper support, sinks at last into a desperate struggle with pessimism, or yields to the easy logic of the Epicurean. Genuine religion demands an even balance of the two, or, more strictly speaking, *is* such a balance. And so in times when the tendency prevails to lose sight of the reality of the otherworld and to seek for the basis of ethics in purely natural grounds, the office of wisdom would be, by every available use of the imagination and a chastened reason, to revivify the soul's inborn conviction that its veritable life is not in this world of physical things—that above all, whatever else may follow. Only so can the effective balance of religion be restored and an adequate counterweight be found to the imperious will of the

flesh. Unless the sense of spiritual values be
somehow reawakened, I do not see what power
shall check the visibly growing empire of materialism with the restlessness of mind that seeks
relief in mere dissipation. Art will not do it,
science will not do it, the sociology of brother-
hood will not do it, while against the immediate
lure of pleasure the positive weighing of consequences offers but a feeble defence. Only by the
power of a higher desire can the lower desires be
kept within bounds.

In Platonism the emphasis lies heavily on the
union of otherworldliness and morality in the
philosophy of Ideas. That is the beginning of
religion, its anchor, its hope, its last refuge of
assurance; it carries, Plato would say, its own
irrefragable conviction to the open and seeing
mind, and requires no testimony in revelation.
It is, if both are rightly understood, in harmony
with the great faith of the Orient, and might
not improperly be called a poetical version of
the Buddhistic doctrine of Karma; it has given,
and always will give, the assurance of faith to
the true sceptic. The risk of such a philosophy is
that it may not grasp the personality of God
and the existence of free spirits in the world of
Ideas, and so, through an imperfect theology

and mythology, may become inhuman and more speculative than practical. Christianity, though among the wiser doctors it never loses its grasp of the Platonic Idealism, takes its start not in philosophy but in mythology, and draws its confidence from the revelation of a personal God through the historic event, or, if you choose so to regard it, the dogma, of the Incarnation. In that union of two natures, divine and human, in one person a complete philosophy will discern, enacted as it were in a cosmic drama, the last expression of the mystery, the beginning of which lies in the dualism of mind and matter.

CHAPTER II

THE PREPARATION OF ISRAEL

WHEN Jesus returned to Galilee after his baptism in the Jordan he began to preach the gospel as he had heard it announced by John: "The time is fulfilled, and the kingdom of God is at hand, repent"; or, as the words are elsewhere reported: "Repent, for the kingdom of heaven is at hand." That was the heart of the new evangel; and in those two terms, "the kingdom" and "repentance," we have the specifically Christian form of the constant factors of religion: otherworldliness and morality. Of this there can be no doubt. But of the exact meaning to be attached to these two terms and of the relation of Jesus himself to the kingdom and to repentance, question may very well arise; indeed the whole dispute of modern theology turns on the solution of this problem.

Evidently the first point to consider in arriving at our judgement of the gospel will be the tradi-

Mk. 1, 15

Mt. iv, 17

tional view of these matters held at the time of
Christ's ministry: what was the notion of the
kingdom and of repentance inherited by the
Jews from their long antecedent history?

Now from the days of the exodus out of
Egypt to the time when the Roman soldiers
under Titus overthrew the Temple and left the
people without a centre of rallying and without
reasonable hope of recovery, for some thirteen
centuries, the annals of Israel record a bitter and
almost continuous struggle, alternating with
elation and dejection, to preserve intact her na-
tionality. About the intruders who scattered
themselves along the short river in Palestine
from lake to lake, were hostile tribes and peoples,
whose animosity was not the less savage when
kinship of race existed between them. There
were successive wars of extermination, which
never quite exterminated, and for a while, under
David and Solomon, the promise of a great Hebrew empire. But to the East was growing up
the power of another Semitic people in Assyria,
extending its borders step by step, with desolat-
ing regularity, until in the eighth century the
northern province of Samaria was devastated,
and, in 701, Sennacherib, king of Nineveh, fell
upon Jerusalem "like the wolf on the fold."

Precisely one hundred years after that Judea was submitting to Nebuchadnezzar, lord of the succeeding empire of Chaldea. Then came the ruin of Jerusalem, and the exile, when the king and the principal men of the city were carried off to the Euphrates. For half a century Israel was virtually absorbed in the Chaldean empire, when for some reason the power of the Semites began to wane and the long domination of the Aryans set in. In 538 Babylon was conquered by Cyrus, and under the milder sway of Persia the Jews were permitted gradually to return to their homes. These were the wonderful years of the restoration; the Temple is rebuilt, the old worship is restored, and for a while it looks as if the little community about Jerusalem might enjoy the peace and security of a theocratic state untroubled by the welter of the world. But not for long. Internal dissension breaks out, the overweening pride of the prosperous and the worldly ambition of the priesthood crush the humbler classes, and hope turns to bitterness. Alexander of Macedon takes the land on his triumphant march to Egypt; at the turn of the third century Palestine becomes a portion of the Greco-Syrian rule of the Seleucids at Antioch, a rule broken for a time by the fierce revolt of the

Maccabees, then renewed and confirmed, until the Romans, the real kings of men, sweep Greek and Syrian and Hebrew into the one vast empire.

How the Jews persisted as a nation through these vicissitudes of fortune is one of the miracles of history. But, granted that power of endurance and cohesion, whatever its source, it is not strange that, through the pressure of such events, the feeling of racial singularity, the faith in themselves as a people set apart for a divine destiny, should have become intensely acute. We can see this hardening of national consciousness in two lines of growth, which sometimes run together, but at other times are distinct if not openly antagonistic. On the one side stands the Law, or Thorah, that body of meticulous precepts regulating every act of worship and controlling the whole outward conduct of a man. In its inception the law of the Israelites was very similar to that prevailing among the nations, particularly the Semitic tribes, about them. But in the course of time it expanded and became more national. Especially during the Babylonian captivity and in the enthusiasm of the restoration it fell under the influence of priestly scribes and was codified and intertwined with a semi-mythical history of the people in the form which it now presents in the Pentateuch. Later, as we see in the *Book of Jubilees,* one of the so-called apocalyptic works composed towards the end of the second century B.C., it was held that the complete Law was written down by Moses on Mount Sinai at the dictation of the Lord or of "the angel of the presence." As such it was eternal in its validity, enduring from the beginning of time to the end, and possessed with a kind of mystical power which should gradually transform the earth into a heavenly paradise.

The other line of national development, now running parallel with the legalistic and now crossing it, was through the voice of prophecy. From the beginning there were seers and soothsayers in Israel as in all primitive peoples, men who claimed a special knowledge of the divine oracles and signs; but the school of prophets who added a new note to the religion of Israel and of the world, and whose message forms a special part of the canonical Scriptures, begins with the shepherd Amos, who, in the eighth century, went up from the pasture land of Tekoa to the royal sanctuary of Bethel with his denunciations of coming doom, proceeds on to Daniel and to the anonymous writers of the Greek period whose sentences have been merged into the works of their more famous predecessors, and still on to the so-called apocalyptic and eschatological[1] authors of the Maccabean and Roman ages whose books were not admitted into the body of canonical Scripture.

In one thing all these prophets agree: they speak in the name of Jehovah, as do the makers and interpreters of the Law. But the God whose spokesman they profess to be has undergone a remarkable change. At the beginning Jehovah is not much more than the tribal Lord of Israel, one, though a greater one, among the Baals of the various peoples, and his worship may be described as a jealous monolatry. But with the years His power and majesty enlarge until His name becomes synonymous with deity and the religion of Israel breaks forth as a pure mono-
Is. xliv, 6 theism: "I am the first and I am the last, and

---

[1] Apocalyptic books are those that contain a revelation or vision expressed in symbolical form. They are also eschatological when the revelation is concerned with the "Last Things," the end of the present world-order and the institution of the celestial age. Parts of the canonical prophets, e g., Isaiah, are both apocalyptic and eschatological. In the last three centuries of Israel's existence as a nation there grew up a considerable literature of this character. It was commonly fathered upon one of the ancient sages or prophets. Daniel, which is of this order and became current in the second century B.C., was incorporated in the canonical body of Scripture, but the other books have been left as apocrypha. Eschatology, the science of the "Last Things," is a word of which we shall have to make much use.

beside Me there is no God." It would not be
fair to ascribe this extraordinary development
altogether to the preaching of the individual
prophets, for, after all, they were children of
their people; but they were the voice of the nation, often an admonitory and hostile voice, and
one cannot read the great chapters of prophecy
without feeling that to Isaiah and his compeers
had been granted a vision of the divine nature
such as can be found in no other books of the
world. A breath of inspiration pulsates through
their words, at times so clear and pure and high
that even today the hearer is awed, and says to
himself: This is the very oracle of God.

There is no inherent antipathy between the
prophetic and the legalistic conception of Jehovah, and in its later codification the Law has
eliminated the notion of a tribal deity for a universal monotheism. And essentially there is no
moral antipathy. Though the Law of necessity
expressed its precepts chiefly in the form of negation, it was able in the Ten Commandments
to assimilate the morality of the prophets, and
in its Great Commandment of love it anticipated, as we shall see, the spirit of the New Testament. But practically and as interpreted at times
by a worldly priesthood, the Law did lend itself

to dead legalism against which the prophets in-
veighed, often with bitterness. Against the undue insistence on the forms of worship they had
to protest that Jehovah was the Lord of life
rather than of custom. "For I desire love and
not sacrifice," was the word as it came through
Hosea, "and the knowledge of God more than
burnt offerings"; and again: "What doth Jehovah require of thee, but to do justly, and to
love mercy, and to walk humbly with thy God?"
To sum up we may say that, though the Law, as
it was finally codified in the canonical books, contains much of pure worship, much that incul-
cates a sound morality, yet in the main the tendency was to identify religion with the customs
which distinguished Israel from the rest of the
world, and to substitute the letter of precept
for the freedom of spirit. Meanwhile, beside the
written code, minute enough in itself, was growing up a vast jungle of interpretations and traditions, which only the few could know and still
fewer carry out. The result at the last was a division between the "righteous" and the "sinners"
not unlike the caste system of India which separated the Brahmins from the rest of the people.
Against all this the prophets in their age pro-
tested, as Jesus also was to do.

vi, 6

Mic. vi, 8

The ethical note alters little from prophet to prophet. And on another point they were all agreed: with one voice they call for repentance as the means of introducing Jehovah's visible reign upon earth. As power after power breaks into the defenceless territory of the Jordan, through the successive terrors of devastation, through defeat and victory, captivity and restoration, the intense nationalism of Israel, as it finds utterance in the prophetic voices, is insistent on this one truth, that the calamities, whether threatened or actual, are owing to the evil-doing of the people or of their rulers, that the only hope of safety lies in repenting and in turning again to the God of righteousness, and that now or afterwards Jehovah will show mercy to His elect and establish them in an empire that shall endure to the end of the world.

The summons to contrition, as the basis of morality acceptable to God, persists throughout the centuries; it is the same cry ever repeated: "Turn ye now from your evil ways," "Return unto me and I will return unto you, saith Jehovah." But the associated idea of the kingdom grows larger and more elevated, though its progress suffers occasional check and relapse. From the beginning the reign of Jehovah has a double

Zech. i, 4
Mal. iii, 7

aspect, corresponding, one might say, to the inevitable contrast between the actual and the ideal. Thinking of the majesty and unchanging power of God the Jew was bound to contemplate the world, or at least his own territory, as now and always under the divine sway; but when he looked at the actual state of Palestine and the heathen peoples about him, then the ideal vanished, and he pictured the kingdom of God only as a blessing always to come, yet still deferred, waiting always upon the conversion and penance of the chosen race. Naturally at the first, under the fierce rivalry of tribal settlement, the future kingdom appeared as a victorious and vengeful Israel, which had established itself by blood and massacre, as Jehovah had once commanded Saul I Sam. xv, 3 to slay the Amalekites, "both man and woman, child and suckling, ox and sheep, camel and ass." And then, as the years passed, and the promise of peace was not fulfilled, and Israel, now an established nation, came into conflict with the larger empires of Asia, the still expected kingdom assumed a correspondingly larger aspect. The longing for vengeance and the hope of national triumph remained, but against the weight of such foes something more was needed than the bare sword of Israel; the very hand of Je-

hovah should be stretched out upon the world,
to smite the presumptuous despots with pesti-
lence and famine and confusion, until they
bowed the neck to the Lords of Jerusalem. And
still the hour of triumph was deferred. The sense
of guilt and of responsibility for the delay struck
deeper into the heart of Israel, and the desire of
revenge is modified to a thought of doom impending upon the whole world. For a season the
voice of the Lord might yet be heard, pleading
with all people, Jew and gentile alike, to repent:
"Turn unto me and be delivered, all ye ends of   Is. xiv, 22
the earth! For I am God and there is none else.
By Myself I have sworn, . . . that unto me
every knee shall bow, every tongue shall swear."
But the call goes unheeded, and wickedness mul-
tiplies; the day of vengeance breaks, and Jehovah tramples upon the nations of the earth as
a man treads in a wine-trough alone:

> I trod down the peoples in mine anger,   Is. lxiii, 6
> And crushed them in my fury,
> And poured out their life-blood on the ground.

Out of the remnant of Israel a new people of
Zion shall be gathered, and out of the remnant
of the gentiles new nations who shall come up
to Jerusalem yearly to share in the worship of   Zech. xiv, 16
the everlasting God. Thus shall the justice and

righteousness of Jehovah be vindicated at the
last, and from the rising of the sun even to its
going-down His name shall be magnified.

So, through the long years of disappointment, the hope of a narrow military and political triumph was widened to a vision embracing
the world; and from this to a purely apocalyptic
view of the great day of Jehovah is an easy transition, when indeed the two are not blended indis-
tinguishably together. It is no longer the peoples
of the earth only who dree their weird before
the eyes of the prophets; the event becomes cosmic, commencing with catastrophes that shake
the foundations of the visible universe and end-
ing with a renewal of all things under the beni-
son of God's mercy. For the wise there shall be
signs of the coming doom:

And I will show portents in heaven and earth;
Blood and fire and pillars of smoke.
The sun shall be turned into darkness, and the moon into
    blood,
Before the coming of the great and terrible day of Jehovah.

Then the hand of the Lord shall smite once and
smite again:

And the mountains shall be melted with their blood,
And all the host of heaven shall be dissolved.
The skies shall be rolled together as a scroll,

Mal. 1, 11

Joel ii, 30

Is. xxxiv, 3-8

And all their host shall perish with age. . . .
For Jehovah hath a day of vengeance.

In that day the nations of earth shall be brought together to the Valley of Jehoshaphat, "noisy multitudes, noisy multitudes in the valley of decision," until the word of judgement has silenced them for ever. When the tumult is stilled and the dooms have been pronounced, then the earth shall be a new paradise upon which the gladness and glory of heaven have descended, and from the Mount of Zion the chosen of the Lord shall rule in unbroken peace.

Joel iii, 14

There is not much change from the vision of the later canonical prophets to the eschatology of the pseudonymous writers that follow. Perhaps the influence of Persian dualism, which is already felt in Daniel, becomes more marked. The political, even the human, aspect of the events fades a little more into the background, and what was sublime and terrible tends to fantastic exaggeration. In one book at least the sins and abominations of the world are attributed to those angels, the children of heaven, who saw and lusted after the comely daughters of men. But through all this overgrowth of the supernatural the old hopes of national and material prosperity are not forgotten, nor is the fierce

Enoch vi

spirit of patriotism quenched. In an early portion of the Fourth Book of Ezra, composed not much before the fall of Jerusalem, possibly during the life of Christ, the vision of Daniel is recalled; though now the "fourth beast, dreadful and terrible, fearful, and strong exceedingly," which in Daniel had symbolized the Greco-Macedonian Empire, is converted into the eagle of Rome whose wings are outspread over the whole world; and the lion of Judah who utters a man's voice against the eagle and pronounces its doom is "the Messiah whom the Most High hath kept unto the end of the days, who shall spring from the seed of David."

vii, 7

xii, 32

From the beginning to the end the expectation of the kingdom was associated with the Messiah, that is "the anointed one," or, as the word appears in Greek, the Christ; but naturally with the varying conceptions of the kingdom, the divinely appointed ruler therein assumes different forms. Commonly he was prophesied to be of the legitimate line of David, of the tribe of Judah and out of the root of Jesse; though at one time, under the hopes raised by John Hyrcanus towards the close of the second century B.C., Messianic hymns were addressed to that leader as an offshoot of the tribe of Levi. When

the narrower views of nationalism prevailed the
Messiah sprung from David appeared as an
ordinary monarch, though even so it was the
outstretched hand of Jehovah that should guide
to victory:

There shall come forth a sprout from the stock of Jesse,   Is. xi, 1
And a branch out of his roots shall bear fruit.
The spirit of Jehovah shall rest upon him,
A spirit of wisdom and understanding. . . .
And he shall smite the earth with the rod of his mouth,
And with the breath of his lips shall he slay the wicked.

At other times the direct lordship of God was
still more emphasized, and the earthly potentate
sinks into insignificance. Or where the Messiah
maintains his importance, he is caught up into
the cosmic and eschatological vision, and becomes a mysterious figure, half human, half
godlike, king at once and celestial judge, who
shall appear with the thunder and doom of universal catastrophe, and whose throne shall be on
earth and in the courts of heaven.

Of special significance, owing to the use of
the phrase in the New Testament, is the designation of the Messiah as the Son of man. Now
in themselves these words are merely the ordinary Hebrew or Aramaic idiom for "man," as
may be seen, for instance, in the familiar pas-

Ps. viii, 14 sage: "What is man that thou art mindful of him, or the son of man that thou visitest him?" But it is clear also that from an early date the appellation acquired a certain solemnity of association, and stood often as an abbreviation for some such phrase as "the man of God," "the man of heaven," "the first man," or the like. In this way it came to be appropriated by the prophets as symbolical of their mediatorial office between man and God. So in Ezekiel the title is chosen by Jehovah for the messenger through whom the divine admonitions are conveyed, while it suggests also a personification of iii, 4 the whole race for whom he mediates: "And he said unto me, Son of man, go, get thee unto the house of Israel, and speak with my words unto them." From Ezekiel it is not a far step to Daniel, where the phrase first appears in extant literature with its full figurative meaning. Here in contrast to the four bestial empires of the heathen the Jewish people is portrayed in the semblance of a glorified humanity, as the Son of man coming before the Ancient of Days "with" or "on" the clouds. To him, as the personified Israel, were given "dominion and glory, and sovereignty, that all the peoples, nations, and languages should serve him; and his domin-

ion is an everlasting dominion which shall not
pass away, and his sovereignty that which shall
not be destroyed."

But the important change for history comes
with the transference of the appellation from the
people of the kingdom to the anointed ruler.
Whether the phrase was taken by later apocalyptic writers from Daniel and consciously re-
interpreted or came to them ready to hand with
this different sense from a parallel tradition, we
cannot say. So far as the literature is preserved
we find the identification first made in the book
of Enoch, and in a manner which might suggest
that the new usage took its rise from a blend of
Ezekiel and Daniel. As in Ezekiel, here the
messenger who reveals the hidden things of Jehovah to the people is a prophet, Enoch; but as
in Daniel he has himself become a mythical figure and is brought into the presence of the Head
of Days, whose "head was white like wool."
And there he beholds the Son of man in the
full blaze of apocalyptic and eschatological
glory, as the "anointed," "the world judge," the
"world-ruler," he to whom Jehovah can say
"My Son":

At that hour that Son of man was named   xlviii, 2
In the presence of the Lord of Spirits,

And his name before the Head of Days.

Yea, before the sun and the signs were created,

Before the stars of the heaven were made,

His name was named before the Lord of Spirits.

He shall be a staff to the righteous whereon to stay themselves and not fall,

And he shall be the light of the gentiles,

And the hope of those who are troubled of heart.

All who dwell on earth shall fall down and worship before
him,

And will praise and bless and celebrate with song the Lord
of Spirits.

And for this reason hath he been chosen and hidden before
Him,

Before the creation of the world and for evermore.

Such, in brief, was the development of the conceptions of the divine kingdom and repentance,
of the Messiah and the Son of man, through the
long weary course of Israel's struggle to maintain herself. With that background in view we
can understand the various parties that divided
the nation when Jesus was born in Nazareth. On
one side was the politically dominant sect of
Sadducees, who clung to the letter of the Law
and denied the newer doctrine of the resurrection. Against them stood the Pharisees, who accepted the resurrection but overlaid the Mosaic
code with extravagant traditions and burden-

some interpretations. History also tells us something of the party of Zealots, for whom the promised son of David was to be a warrior king who should smite the pride of Rome and raise Israel to independence, if not to the hegemony of the world. As for the eschatological beliefs at the time there was probably diversity of opinion with varying degrees of faith. To some extent the dualism of Persia, with its hostile ranks of good and evil spirits and its contrasted worlds of light and darkness, had certainly permeated the imagination of the whole people. But the more fantastic visions of the post-canonical writers remained, I think, the delectation of the few and the sport of the rabbinical schools. Everything in the Gospels would indicate that the prevalent spiritual force of the age is to be found in the scriptural prophets. It is they that were read and expounded in the synagogues; it is they that stood by the side of the books of the Law as the recognized oracles of Jehovah; it is they, visionary enough yet for the most part sober in comparison with the later works, that must have moulded the thoughts of Jesus himself, giving to him his ideas of the kingdom and repentance, and of the elect of God, who, after the stilling of the terrible "Messianic woes" and the passing of judgement, should rule over a newly created world of peace and good will.

So far the "Christological problem" might seem to present no great difficulty, and, in fact, I suppose there would be no problem at all, were it not for the acute question of the relation of Jesus himself to these matters. Undoubtedly he announced the Messianic kingdom, but did he announce himself as the Messiah? One can see that this is a question of profound import, and that a man's answer to it might cause him, by a kind of reflex action, to adopt views of the kingdom and of repentance which otherwise would never have occurred to his mind. One can see too that our position here will depend largely on our critical attitude to the documents which pretend to give a record of Christ's life and teaching, unless it happens conversely that our attitude to the documents is governed by a preconception of what his life and teaching must have been. At any rate the Christological problem and the literary problem cannot be severed; we cannot form any tenable opinion about the character of Christ without determining how far we shall admit the evidence of the Gospels as historical.

Now we must begin by simply waiving the

old-fashioned orthodox view, at least in its more
intransigent form. To take the books of the
New Testament as verbally inspired, to overlook their manifest incoherences and contradictions, and to find in them only what a childlike
faith demands, may be edifying, but is no longer
possible for anyone who knows what has been
written and thought on the subject.[2]

On the other hand I think we may pay no
heed to the vociferous band led by W. B. Smith
in America, J. M. Robertson in England, and
A. Drews in Germany, who are reducing Christianity to pure myth and symbolism, with no
vital relation to the teaching of a man Jesus, if
indeed such a man ever existed. It is a lusty band,
and makes pretensions to enormous erudition
in the widening field of comparative religion;
but its champions, as I am bound to think, are
shockingly defective in the saving grace of common sense. By their methods of proof any field
of history might be transformed to an amusing
fairy tale. For my part I cannot take their thesis
seriously; of any group of scholars who deny, or

[2] I write this though I have Papini's *Storia di Cristo* before me,
with these words of the introduction staring me in the face: *Chi
accetta i quattro Evangeli deve accettarli tutti interi, sillaba per
sillaba*—and he accepts them, every syllable. The book is a despi-
cable piece of work, calculated in the end, I think, to do the
Christian religion no good.

virtually deny, the existence of the man Jesus, I
can only say:

Of them we will not speak, but look and pass.

The one solid rock on which we have to build
is the authenticity of the major epistles of Paul,
including the First Thessalonians, First and
Second Corinthians, Galatians, and Romans.
Except for a few extreme radicals, whose views
are coloured by transparent preconceptions and
are not supported by any valid arguments, these
epistles today are universally accepted as genuine. Our position would not be affected by
omitting Second Thessalonians, Philippians,
and Colossians, which are disputed, although
the weight of evidence is strong in their favour.
Next it is to be remembered that the writer of
these letters was converted within five years,
probably only one year after the crucifixion. Before his conversion he had been an ardent enemy
of the Christians. He was deeply learned in the
Law, a man absorbed in religion, and it is inconceivable that he should have entered on a
course of persecution without clear grounds for
doing so. Paul's hostility was kindled against
the new sect because they held that Jesus, a man
who had suffered the ignominy of the cross, was

the Messiah of prophecy and had so proclaimed himself to his disciples. This, then, is the historic fact from which we start: soon, not many months, after the death of Jesus his disciples believed that he had claimed to be the Christ of prophecy. That is certain. The presumption is very strong that he did make such a claim.

By this presumption the question of the authenticity of the synoptic Gospels loses its chief difficulty; for most of the objections raised against them have sprung from an obstinate determination to escape just this conclusion of Jesus' Messianic teaching and consciousness. No valid reason remains for scepticism. And in fact it is fair to say that the consensus of unbiassed scholars is veering steadily to the belief that Mark (written probably just before the destruction of Jerusalem in A.D. 70) and the so-called Q (*i.e., Quelle,* "source," a lost document on which Matthew and Luke drew for the sayings of Jesus common to them and not found in Mark) are essentially trustworthy. For my part I can see no reason to suspect the tradition reported by Papias and Irenaeus in the second century that Mark acted as Peter's interpreter in Rome and "delivered to us in writing the things which had been preached by Peter"; nor any good reason for rejecting the other tradition that the Apostle Matthew made a collection of Christ's Logia, or sayings, with the inference that the Q of Luke and of the present Gospel of Matthew goes back to that document. But the acceptance or rejection of these traditions should not be allowed to affect the fundamental fact that the kernel of the synoptic Gospels, that is to say the Messianic setting for the preaching of the kingdom, agrees with the earliest belief of the Church as we know it from Paul's epistles. The clearest conception of the course of Jesus' life as the self-proclaimed Messiah can be drawn from Mark, and this is natural since he is nearest in date to the events. His account shows some chronological confusion, and even Papias admits that he did not write in an orderly manner; but on the whole he makes the impression of a fairly intelligent witness. The narrative of Mark, as it is taken over into Matthew and Luke, shows evident manipulation and loses progressively in coherence. The problem of John is of a different order and does not concern us here.

This is the eschatological theory of Paul and the Gospels which, like the wind and rain of the parable, is beating down the stronghold of the so-called Liberal Protestantism. Much learning

has been expended on the theology of the older
school, it still has great advocates in and out of
Germany; but it was doomed from the beginning for the reason that it is builded on sand.
Its foundation is in these two presuppositions:
that nothing supernatural can be true, and that
Jesus was the spirit of truth. It concludes therefore that Jesus could not have made any supernatural claims for himself. Now as regards the
supernatural, we may or may not reject that
out of hand as incredible, though we should be
growing a little more cautious in our definition
of what is "natural"; but to infer from the second thesis that Christ must have spoken of himself as a mere man, inspired, perhaps, with an
extraordinary sense of the Fatherhood of God,
yet with no claim to miraculous authority,—to
argue on such an inference means that we are
allowing a dubious psychology to override the
critical weighing of evidence. Certainly the burden of proof bears heavily upon the liberal theologians. Confronted with the testimony in Paul
and Mark, they reply that no doubt Jesus announced the coming of the kingdom and of *a*
Messiah, but never announced himself as *the*
Messiah. The confusion of *a* and *the* took place
in the Church after his death, when the disciples,

raised to a state of exaltation by the supposed reappearance of their Master, transferred to Jesus himself the prophecies he had made of another, and so gradually transfigured him in their imagination to the glorified Christ. The explanation is ingenious, but highly improbable. In the vulgar metaphor, it puts the cart before the horse; for by any sound canon of criticism we should suppose that the memory of their leader's claims was the cause of their belief in his Resurrection, not the reverse. It is not easy to account for that belief on any other ground, unless indeed we accept the Resurrection as a supernatural fact, which of course the "liberal theologian" cannot do.

There is something pathetic in the effort of these scholars to preserve Christianity as a comforting faith while depriving it of any supernatural basis. The theory of a purely humanitarian Saviour, when presented with the sincerity of Harnack's *What is Christianity?*, possesses a certain charm and winsomeness; but there is no real driving force behind it, nothing that will long satisfy the craving heart of man, nothing to which the spirit may cling when the waves of worldliness and materialism are beating about it on every side. And in the hands of

lesser men the theory becomes a mere travesty
of religion. "It was a gospel of glad tidings for
the poor," writes a learned professor of the liberal school in this country, "an easy yoke in place
of the grievous burdens of the scribes, rest for
weary souls—and yet withal a higher righteousness than the Pharisaic morality. . . . Cham-
pion of the 'lost sons' he cannot and will not
cease to be. Against the hierocracy in Jerusalem such championship, in spite of Jesus' best
endeavours against misinterpretation, could not
fail to undergo suffusion with the glamour of
Messianism."[3] When theology can find only this
in the life of Jesus, it is no longer moribund, but
dead, or at least the religion it advocates is dead.
And when scholarship, in its abhorrence of the
supernatural, goes so far as to maintain that
the synoptic Jesus "never overstepped the limits
of the purely human,"[4] it has simply committed
suicide, poisoned itself in its own prejudices.

We are left, then, with these solid facts: that
Jesus lived and taught in Palestine, and suffered
death on the cross; that he preached repentance
in view of the imminence of the kingdom of God;
and that, in the tradition of the earliest Chris-

[3] B. W. Bacon, *Beginnings of Gospel Story*, xxxix.
[4] W. Bousset, *Jesus*, trans. by J. P. Trevelyan, 202.

tians, he announced himself as the Messiah, or Christ, who should reign there under God. The presumption that his disciples were not mistaken in their belief and that Jesus did so announce himself, is so strong that only a wilful prejudice can question it.

CHAPTER III

THE EARLY YEARS

IT is possible that Jesus, while announcing himself as the Messiah, was merely an impostor and had in his mind no such thought about himself. But this view runs so counter to the note of sincerity in his life and words that it has never entered seriously into the consideration of critics; it may be dismissed as incredible. The question then will be how he came to believe in his supernatural function and in what way he revealed the belief. And to this question three answers are current:

(1) He was fully conscious of a divine charge and from the beginning of his ministry gave expression to the fact clearly and categorically. Such a theory fits the record of John and in part that of Matthew and Luke, but can scarcely be reconciled with Mark's more probable version of the story. And there are other obvious difficulties in the way of accepting it.

(2) He possessed complete consciousness of
his nature from the beginning, but revealed himself only gradually and in glimpses; full knowledge was to be given with the coming of the
Holy Ghost. This explanation accords well
enough with the synoptical narratives and can
be forced upon John. Chrysostom has developed
the thesis with masterly skill in his sermons on
Matthew, and in general it has found acceptance
among the more orthodox theologians. But
again there are difficulties. How and when did
this perfect self-consciousness arise in his mind?
Suddenly at the moment of baptism, shall we
say, thus making a complete break between the
first thirty or more years of his life and the brief
period of his ministry? That surely is not probable. Or shall we suppose that he was fully aware
of his mission from infancy? That is more than
unlikely, it is unthinkable. Attractive as this
hypothesis has been to a certain type of commentator, it must yield to another view of the
matter, viz.:

(3) Jesus in his early years had no fully
formed sense of his mission, but with time and
experience grew to an ever clearer, yet possibly
never perfectly defined, self-consciousness. Only
this hypothesis can be made to harmonize with

the synoptical record, especially with Mark, and at the same time with the working of an intelligence limited by the conditions of mortal existence.

Nor is it difficult, or presumptuously daring, to trace the larger steps by which such a man as Jesus, aware from childhood of peculiar powers and of some mystical urgence within his soul, came to regard himself as the divinely appointed Messiah of his people, even perhaps as the Saviour of the world. Though Joseph was only a carpenter in the provincial town of Nazareth, there is no good reason to discredit the tradition that the family held itself to be of the ancient lineage of David.[1] One can imagine the thoughts of a boy in such a household, through whose members, to judge from the later history

[1] Dalman is perfectly sound in his interpretation of the vexed passage, Mat. xxii, 45; Mark xii, 37; Luke xx, 44: "In his question how the Lord of David could be David's son, Jesus showed that the corporal descent from David had no significance for the being of the Messiah. It does not follow from this text that the supposed Davidic descent was not the cause of his occupying himself with the thought of the Messiahship. Moreover it is quite in keeping with his whole view of the position of the Messiah that only God could appoint to that office" (*Die Worte Jesu*, 262). The claim of Jesus' family to Davidic descent was known to Paul, and could not have been manufactured by the Church at that early date when the brothers of Jesus were still living. And we know from Hegesippus (Eusebius, *Ec. Hist.* iii, 19, 20) that Domitian had members of the family brought to Rome to investigate their claims to the kingship of the Jews.

of his brothers, ran a vein of religious fervour:
how he would brood on the fallen state of his
people Israel, the repeated insults of the foreign-
ers to the worship of Jehovah; how then he would
turn with equal indignation to the evils at home,
the pride of the Pharisees who had identified religion with the exactions of a law so hard and
complicated that the mass of the people, including his own family, was left to perish as impure
"sinners." Was not this the outer and the inner
wrong which had been denounced by the prophets, from the day seven long centuries past when
Amos had foretold the vengeance of God upon
the three transgressions, yea four, of the op-
pressors of Israel, and upon the three transgressions, yea four, of Israel himself? Should the divine patience endure for ever? Was the hour at
last come when Jehovah should utter His voice
from Zion and pour out His devouring fires?
And if the day was about to break upon the un-
believing world when every man, whether Jew
or gentile, should be called to account, the dead
from their hiding place together with the living,
what part was he to take in the drama of resti-
tution, he, Jesus the son of Joseph, of the stock
of Jesse? A youth's thoughts are long, long
thoughts:—

When I was yet a child, no childish play
To me was pleasing; all my mind was set
Serious to learn and know, and thence to do
What might be public good; myself I thought
Born to that end, born to promote all truth,
All righteous things: therefore above my years
The law of God I read, and found it sweet.[2]

It does not seem over-adventurous to read such musings into the early years of Jesus, and to imagine him so listening to the inner call and hesitating, yet knowing amid his doubts that one day he must go forth, whether to preach or to act. On him rested the promise given to the royal line; in his heart the prophetic voice was whispering; when would the call ring clear and loud? Now he could only say: "Alas, O Lord Jehovah! behold I do not know how to speak, for I am but a youth." Some day he should hear the command, as it had been heard by Ezekiel: "Son of man, seest thou what the elders of the house of Israel are doing? . . . Therefore, thou Son of man, prophesy, and smite thine hands together. . . . And when it cometh to pass—lo, it will come!—then they shall know that a prophet was among them."

Meanwhile there ran through Galilee the rumour of a new prophet who had arisen in Israel

Jer. 1, 6

viii, 12
xxi, 14
xxxiii, 33

2 *Paradise Regained*, i, 201 et seqq.

and was stirring the hearts of the people with fear and hope. In the lonely land about the Jordan, north of Jerusalem and east of Jericho, John was living, clad in rough garments like Elijah of old (or Elias as he is commonly called in the New Testament), and eating the natural food of the desert, as it were one crying in the wilderness: "Repent and be baptized, for the kingdom of God is at hand; make ready the way of the Lord, for he cometh who is greater than I, and whose baptism shall be in the holy spirit, as mine is only of water." There was nothing startlingly original—how should there be?—in John's union of repentance with baptism; the act meant for him the purification first of the soul with the waters of justice and chastity, followed by the symbolic washing of the body.[3] The same association of ideas had coloured the language of the prophets:

Is. 1, 16   Wash you, and make you clean.
Put away the evil of your doings from before mine eyes.
Cease to do evil; learn to do well;
Seek justice; relieve the oppressed;
Vindicate the orphan; plead for the widow.

Washing and sprinkling were an integral part of Jewish ceremony, and among the Essenes of

[3] Josephus, *Ant.*, XVIII, v, 2.

John's time the practice of frequent baptism was carried to a fantastic excess. Indeed, whether as a symbol or as a sacrament with magic efficacy, the rite is likely to be adopted wherever the conscience is troubled by the stains of violence and impurity. With John himself the act probably had the further significance of marking and sealing the baptized for acceptance in the approaching kingdom; and by the Christians after the death of Christ it was taken over from John's partisans as a mystical initiation into the Church.

To this oracle in the wilderness men were flocking from every quarter of the land, some to confess their sins and obtain absolution, others to be repulsed with scorn as idlers and hypocrites; and among those who came was Jesus, out of Nazareth. One can imagine him, now in the prime of manhood, standing in the motley crowd, yet isolated by the conscious spirit within him, listening to the fervid ejaculations of the preacher, seeing the waves of excitement pass over the hearers, watching them as they throng down to the cleansing stream of the river. Would he not ask himself whether at last the expected word of direction was given? It was part of the sacred tradition that Elias should appear as a

forerunner of the consummation; and here was
one bearing himself as Elias, having the prophetic power, proclaiming the immediate advent of the kingdom and the King. Was it
possible that John was in truth the expected
prophet, and that he, Jesus of Nazareth, was
none other than the Messiah? How could these
things be, how could they not be? Even today
something like a shudder passes over us at the
thought of the solemn hush and outrushing joy
that must have come upon the spirit of the man
Jesus, as he stood amid the throng of pilgrims,
hearing what seemed to be an answer to the
questioning of his years. In some such mood we
can imagine him presenting himself to the Baptist, and going down into the sacred stream.
And as he emerged from the sacrament it may
be that for an instant everything was clear, that
truth flashed upon him as it were out of the sky:
Mk. 1, 10   "And straightway coming up out of the water,
he saw the heavens opened, and the Spirit like a
dove descending upon him; and there came a
voice from heaven, saying, Thou art my beloved
Son, in whom I am well pleased." Henceforth,
through all doubts and hesitations, triumphs
and exaltations, he should bear the burden of a
double yet united nature: he was still to be the

man of Galilee, subject to the flesh and the liabilities of the fleshly soul, while in him also, equally a member of his conscious personality, was that which answered to the call of the spirit, blending with his lower nature, yet never losing itself therein. He should know by a heightened sense the awful paradox that is at once the sublimity and the despair of all our mortal lives.

As Mark records the story, Jesus, immediately after the baptism, went away into one of the solitary places of the neighbourhood: "and he was there in the wilderness forty days, tempted of Satan." In itself such an act of withdrawal is not remarkable; other men, when the prospect of a great destiny has broken upon them, have done the same thing. Nor need the words "tempted of Satan" excite any wonder. Reflect for a moment what the call must have signified to a sensitive mind, and the force of that trial and its spiritual agony will be plain enough. Buddha, sitting under the Tree of Enlightenment, felt the temptation to surrender himself to the peace of attained Nirvana and to let the world go maddening down its appointed course; is it strange that Jesus should have shrunk from exposing his faith in himself to the taunts and questionings and plaudits of the mob? And suppose even yet that it was all a dream, that he was still only as other men and in no special sense the "beloved Son," and that the voice came not from heaven but was a deception from hell, should he suffer the anguish of disillusion in addition to the peril of public contempt or the no less oppressive responsibility of popular success? It may well be said that he was tempted of Satan.

To the simple statement of Mark the other Synoptists add a detailed account of a triple attack made by the Devil at the end of the forty days, which, whatever its source, presents in striking mythological scenes the sort of trials that must often have assailed the bearer of the Messianic trust. When at last the decision had been reached, the experience of the future may well have come to him foreshadowed by imagination in a brief and vivid drama of the soul. The appeal to change the stones into bread would symbolize the revolt of the natural man against the privations and weariness he was to accept voluntarily as a necessary part of his mission. The taunt on the pinnacle of the temple would condense the impatient longings to convert the sceptical blind hearts of men by some sudden and bewildering demonstration of the truth. The panorama of the kingdoms of the earth from the mountain top would represent the plea of ambition, when a single word might have started a political uprising and rallied the people about him as a national leader. The kingdom of heaven as proclaimed by the prophets was to be the work of Jehovah's hand, while the part of the herald was to await the appointed hour in patience, preaching the law of righteousness and the need of penance; it would be the Devil's voice that called for drastic measures in place of faith and of dependence on the finer precepts of morality.

In some such way the temptations in the wilderness have always been interpreted, as indeed their meaning lies on the surface of the record with a sublime simplicity. Not so often, perhaps, has their universal significance been seen, as an allegory of the three lusts which in later theology summed up the world's methods of attack—the *libido sentiendi,* the *libido sciendi,* and and the *libido dominandi.* He who sets out to search for the kingdom of heaven on this earth will know them, one and all, and will escape their seduction, if he escape, only by a miracle. First and most persistent, the lust of the senses, the inexplicable drag of the flesh and its desires, the thick, heavy pleasures beside which the delights

of the spirit turn thin and pale. And then the
lust of knowledge, the craving to grasp sensu-
ously and to bring into open view the reality of
things that seem always to be vanishing behind
veils of illusion. And the lust of power, whether
it appear as the coarser ambition to dominate
the will of others, or the subtle temptation of
egotism to take the kingdom of heaven by violence and to forgo the finer virtues of patience
and trust. Such temptations do not come to us
today as they appeared to Jesus in the wilderness or as they came to the men of the Middle
Ages. Like the Mephistopheles of Goethe we
say that the refining hand of culture has reached
even to the Devil. But I do not know that we
are much the wiser for our wisdom, or why, admitting as we are wont the existence of a personal spirit of righteousness, we should be so
certain that the spirit of evil suggestions is
fabulous. At any rate it is true:

> *Er ist schon lang' im Fabelbuch geschrieben:*
> *Allein die Menschen sind nichts besser dran;*
> *Den Bösen sind sie los, die Bösen sind geblieben.*[4]

These things are said to have taken place in
Bethany; and if the tradition is correct, John at

Jn. 1, 28

---

[4] "He has long been written down in the book of fables: but men
are none the better for it; the Evil One they are free of, the evil
remain."

the time of the baptism had crossed over into the Peraea, or the eastern side of the Jordan. At any rate he had put himself into the power of Herod Antipas, who was then the ruler of the Peraea and of Galilee, and by Herod was thrown into prison at Machaerus, no doubt to forestall a possible religious and political uprising against Herod's Roman overlords. Later he suffered death. It was after the imprisonment of John that Jesus came out of the wilderness at last with a clear sense of obligation. He had conquered the Tempter, but at a great price; for one can read between the lines, I think, that the charge he accepted was a burden, at times almost an anguish, to him. He was to learn the difference between dreaming of a great spiritual reform and actually contending with the earth-weighted hearts of men. He had been lapped in a life of serene communion with God, but now the voice had been heard, and a hard destiny was thrusting him out into the world to proclaim abroad the vision that might have been a secret comfort. His duty was almost a profanation. After his first public appearance in Capernaum, when he had taught in the synagogue and healed the sick, so that at night all the city thronged about the house where he lay, the record adds:

Mk. 1, 35

"And in the morning, rising up a great while before day, he went out, and departed into a solitary place, and there prayed.

"And Simon and they that were with him followed after him.

"And when they found him, they said unto him, All men seek for thee.

"And he said unto them, Let us go into the next towns, that I may preach there also: for therefore came I forth."

It requires no deep knowledge of the human heart to feel the pathos of that interrupted prayer in the solitude before dawn; and, remembering this scene, one can understand the many expressions of distress, even of irritation, wrung from him during his ministry at the lack of sympathy and the dulness of faith that met him at every step of his way.

These things were in the future, but they cast a light backward upon the temptation; and surely they must have been present to his mind when, returning home, he took up the broken mission of the Baptist. His first words were an echo of what he had heard by the Jordan: "Repent, for the kingdom of heaven is at hand"; and to the end that was his constant text. What, more precisely, did he mean by the kingdom, and by repentance?

CHAPTER IV

THE KINGDOM AND
REPENTANCE

ONE thing may be said with confidence: the great event of the Gospel was now and here. Jesus was indulging in no empty alarm when he declared that the time was completed and the kingdom near at hand. He was not deliberately deceiving his disciples when he assured them more than once that their generation should not pass away before the fulfilment of the promise, and that some of those standing by him should see with their bodily eyes the coming of the visible glory.

This straightforward understanding of Christ's eschatological meaning has not been, and still is not, acceptable to a tender orthodoxy, for the sufficient reason that the promised event did not take place. And so our commentaries are full of attempts to explain away perfectly clear and concrete statements by allegorizing them into a prophecy of the Church which should gradually extend itself over the

world as an *imperium in imperio*. It will not do.
Any one who has read the apologetic literature
must say that the methods of modern criticism
are often beyond his comprehension.

From the beginning, when Amos uttered his
warning:

iv, 12

> Therefore this will I do unto thee, O Israel;
> And, for that I am about to do this unto thee,
> Prepare to meet thy God, O Israel,—

1 Thes. iv, 15 to the days when St. Paul comforted the Christians who grieved for those who had died before
the expected appearance of the Lord, the note
of immediacy is the same. Always the reckoning
is at hand, yet always it is to come as a surprise:
"The day of the Lord so cometh as a thief in the
night; for when they shall say, Peace and safety,
then suddenly destruction cometh upon them."
Paul was merely repeating the eschatology of
the prophets, and between him and them Christ
uttered exactly the same warning: the kingdom
was approaching with the stealth of a robber;
it was by anticipation here and now, yet the
actual day of Jehovah no man knew, neither the
angels in heaven, nor the Son himself,—only the
Father. The importance of that continuity cannot be too much emphasized. Doubtless there
were changes in the eschatology of the Jews

during the course of the centuries; besides the natural development of ideas, we have to weigh the powerful influence of the captivity, which added a whole range of foreign images; but these never supplanted the native tradition, and were never even perfectly assimilated. So too, as we shall see later, Christ himself certainly introduced a new element into the religion of his people; but, again, his eschatology was simply that of his country and his age.

In the same way a good deal has been written about the opposition between the popular hope of a political kingdom and Christ's insistence on a spiritual reign of God in the hearts of men. There was no such opposition as theology loves to draw.[1] The kingdom preached by Christ was

---

[1] Those who would escape the implications of eschatology make a good deal of Christ's saying, Luke xvii, 21: "The kingdom of God is within you." Now, whatever may be the exact meaning of the preposition here translated "within," one thing is clear: the fact that the words are addressed to the Pharisees and the strong eschatological note of the verses immediately following prove that the phrase cannot signify within your hearts as a spiritual possession in distinction to a manifest appearance. Possibly the preposition means simply "among," though I think this is rather forcing the Greek. Possibly the phrase may imply, as Cyril interpreted it, "in your choice and power as something you can grasp." More probably Gunkel (*Die Wirkungen des heiligen Geistes*, 54) is right in connecting the verse in Luke with the similar saying to the Pharisees in Mat. xii, 28: "But if I cast out devils by the Spirit of God, then the kingdom of God is come unto you." The working of the Spirit is the sign of the new age; the kingdom is potentially here with you now, calling in your hearts for repentance, ready to break forth at any moment in power and manifest glory.

at once political and spiritual; and that unquestionably was the form in which it came to him from the moulding hands of prophecy. In one sense Christ's message may be called political, in so far as he distinguished between the oppressed and the oppressor, between the genuinely pious among the people and the pretenders to formal righteousness among the ruling caste. But there is nothing new or revolutionary in that. His denunciation of the scribes and Pharisees, his stern questioning of the rich, merely echo the complaints and invective of prophet after prophet. But in another sense his message was non-political and spiritual. When in Jerusalem he made the memorable retort: "Render to Caesar the things that are Caesar's, and to God the things that are God's," he was eluding the Pharisees and Herodians, who had been sent "to catch him in his words," after a fashion that caused them to slink away in baffled rage. He was also laying down a profound rule of life for the religious of all times and places. But for the faithful about him then and there, he was repeating the constant exhortation of the prophets, that the day of triumph should not be the prize of human hands and mortal wisdom. Not on chariots and horses should Israel rely, not on

Mk. xii, 17

the sword and the arm of soldiers, not on rebellious uprising,—

> Thus saith the Lord Jehovah, the Holy One of Israel: Is. xxx, 15
> By sitting still and resting shall ye be saved,
> In quietness and in confidence shall be your strength.

Then, in His good hour, God should send out the
armies of heaven, and smite the enemy without
and the oppressor within, and gather His people to Himself. Meanwhile the faithful were to
watch always and wait; and this should be their
prayer: "Thy kingdom come, Thy will be done
on earth as it is in heaven."

And the hope, as it was at once political and
spiritual, so appeared now as national and now
as universal, with an ambiguity not easy for us
to comprehend. Jesus came to save the lost house
of Israel. To the Syrophoenician woman who
claimed his healing mercy he could speak in a
manner that after all these years affects the
reader with a shock of dismay: "Let the children   Mk. vii, 27
first be filled, for it is not meet to take the children's bread and to cast it unto the dogs." Commonly in his public preaching also he reserved
the glory of the restoration for the Jews, the
people of Jehovah; yet there are hints here and
there of a different order. It is not, I think, the
gentile Church that put into the mouth of John

Mt. iii,9

the Baptist the threat that God was able of the stones to raise up children to Abraham, or that invented Christ's denunciation of the cities of Palestine, his wonder at the faith of the heathen,

Mt. viii, 10

and his vision of the many coming from the East and the West to sit down with Abraham in the kingdom, while the sons of the covenant are cast out. I suspect that the commands to go out and preach the gospel to all the world, which so offend the higher criticism because they contradict the narrower scope of other passages, do really go back to Christ himself. That paradoxical alternation of nationalism with universalism, of fierce intolerance with the widest spirit of propaganda, runs through the later prophetical books of the Old Testament, and I can see no reason why it should not be expected in the New Testament.

As with the prophets, the institution of the kingdom was to be preceded by wars and rumours of wars, by horror treading upon the heels of horror. The Evil One for a time should

Ez. vii, 23

be let loose, the land should be full of bloody crimes and the city full of violence; when suddenly, without warning, the Messiah should appear from heaven, and at the sound of the trumpet the people of the world should be gath-

ered together for judgement. So far the event
is plain and fairly consistent, but at this point
we encounter difficulties. In the earlier prophets the kingdom was entirely secular and concerned only Jehovah and those who might be
living at the time; the dead were left to their
eternal repose in the dim regions of Sheol. It
required some readjustment of imagery when
belief in the resurrection was imported into this
simple religion of the Semites; but the foreign
ideas were readily assimilated so long as the
scene of judgement and the place of reward
were restricted to this earth, and the dead were
pictured as arising in bodies not essentially different from those of ordinary men. It was another problem, however, when in the course of
time the dualism of Iran filtered into Palestine,
bringing with it the Zoroastrian conception of
the two worlds of light and darkness, peopled
by highly organized ranks of unbodied spirits,
and demanding a whole range of eschatological
scenes for which the simpler mythology of the
Jew had no place. One can see the results of
this Persian influence in Daniel, side by side
with the more primitive ideas. On the one hand
we have pictures of the evolution of empires
drawn from actual history, while almost in the

same breath the stage becomes cosmic, involving the fate of the dead as well as the living:

Dan. xii, 1   "And at that time shall Michael stand up, the great prince which standeth for the children of thy people; and there shall be a time of trouble, such as never was since there was a nation even to that same time: and at that time thy people shall be delivered, every one that shall be found written in the book.

"And many of them that sleep in the dust of the earth shall awake, some to everlasting life, and some to shame and everlasting contempt.

"And they that be wise shall shine as the brightness of the firmament; and they that turn many to righteousness as the stars for ever and ever."

Is the setting for these events on this earth or in the vast spaces of the cosmos? It is not easy to say; and in the later apocalyptic books, such as *Enoch,* the confusion grows even more baffling.

Now the notable fact is that in the days of Christ this contrast, if not downright contradiction, between the native Hebrew beliefs and a more complicated eschatology had not been reconciled, and indeed has persisted to the present day in the Chiliastic views of many churches. Only so, I think, can one explain the vague imagery of the Gospels, whether the vagueness comes, as I suspect it did, from Christ himself, or was created by the misunderstanding of the apostles. Along with references to the imminent coming of the Messiah are set pictures of the far-off consummation of the world and of time; now the kingdom itself and the reign of the elect, with the apostles on their thrones, are laid here upon our solid globe, yet again they seem to float off before our gaze into the aerial regions of the sky and the courts of Jehovah. In general there is such a mingling of the imagery of heaven and earth as defies comprehension. Perhaps the most striking example of what to the modern reader remains an insoluble mystery, is in the words of Jesus at the Last Supper: "Verily I say unto you, I will drink no more of the fruit of the vine, until that day that I drink it new in the kingdom of God." The simple mind of faith may pass over that extraordinary saying without pause; the words mean something, of course, and they make for edification; and beyond that it is not needful to go. Theologians of the liberal stamp would like to reject the verse as spurious, but for the most part dare not do so, since every canon of sound criticism cries for its retention as authentic; hence they have been driven to the strangest devices of symbolical interpretation, Mk. xiv, 25 which have never succeeded in satisfying themselves or any one else. But suppose now that Christ meant what he said to be taken literally; suppose, as seems to be the case, he uttered those memorable words of the Eucharist, conscious of the shadow of death lying upon him! Picture to yourself the Son of man coming back upon the clouds, with the angels of God about him, and then this cup of wine that is to be drunk with the disciples in the new earth and the new heaven! There is no trace of excitement in the record; it merely adds: "And when they had sung an hymn, they went out into the Mount of Olives."

We attribute these incongruities to the imperfect assimilation of foreign ideas, and that is right no doubt in part. But even closer to the heart of Christ's teaching lies the contrast between the introduction of the kingdom and the character of the kingdom itself, which goes back to the early prophecy of Israel. From the beginning the dawn of Jehovah's day, as the prophets saw it, was red with blood and slaughter. So Amos described it:

ix, 1

The rest of them I will slay with the sword,
Not one of them shall escape,
Nor shall any fugitive be delivered from among them.
Though they dig through to Sheol,

> Thence shall mine hand take them;
> And though they climb up to heaven,
> Thence will I bring them down.

And then, when the sword is stayed and vengeance has been sated, the picture suddenly changes to a scene of idyllic peace and pastoral plenty:

> The ploughman shall overtake the reaper,   ix, 13
> And the treader of grapes him that soweth seed;
> And the mountains also shall drop sweet wine,
> And all the hills shall melt [with fatness].

It may be that this last verse is a late addition to Amos, but the truth of the contrast remains the same. It is found in Hosea, where, after the usual signs of the wrath of Jehovah, it is said:

> I will be as dew to Israel;   xiv, 5
> He shall blossom as the lily.

So, in one of the latest passages of the Old Testament, written apparently in the strenuous days of the Maccabees when the ancient nationalism of the Jews had flamed up in fierce insurrection, the same note is struck:

They shall drink their blood like wine,   Zech. ix, 15
They shall be filled with it like the crevices of an altar.
And Jehovah their God shall give them victory in that day.
Like sheep He shall feed them in His land.

Yea, how good and how beautiful shall it be!
Corn shall make the young men flourish, and new wine the
   maidens!

And all through the wonderful visions of Ezekiel and Isaiah the same pastoral imagery is
seen, as it were in the vapour arising from a bath
of blood: "I myself will be the shepherd of my
flock, and I will lead them to pasture," and,
"The wilderness shall become a fertile garden."

Ez. xxxiv, 15

Is. xxxii, 15

   In part this idyllic note may be accidental, de-
riving from the fact that the first of the literary
prophets, Amos, was himself a shepherd who
left his flocks in Tekoa for his mission of national
doom; but in general it is rather, I think, an
echo of the primeval and worldwide dream of a
golden age which gave the Jews the myth of an
earthly Paradise, and which never faded from
their minds through all the centuries of political
turmoil. However that may be, the important
point is that this contrast between the calam-
itous, bloody end of the old world and the idyllic
peace of the new passes straight from the prophets to Christ. This, I think, gives the key to those
parables which liken the kingdom to the activities of the farm and the vineyard, and which have
been wrested by certain critics into evidence that
there was nothing catastrophic in Christ's vision

of the Last Things. The very urgency of the warning is affected by the double tradition. "In those days," it is said, "after that tribulation, Mk. xiii, 24 the sun shall be darkened, and the moon shall not give her light, and the stars of heaven shall fall, and the powers that are in heaven shall be shaken. And then they shall see the Son of man coming in the clouds with great power and glory." We know the source of these images; but how different is what follows: "Now learn a Mk. xiii, 28 parable of the fig tree; When her branch is yet tender, and putteth forth leaves, ye know that summer is near." And like the warning is the command. At one time the order stands: "Take Mk. xiii, 33, 37 ye heed, watch and pray. . . . And what I say unto you I say unto all, Watch." At another time how different: "Consider the lilies of the Mt. vi, 28, 34 field, how they grow; they toil not, neither do they spin. . . . Take therefore no thought for the morrow. . . . Sufficient unto the day is the evil thereof." As for the actual life in the kingdom we find surprisingly few details in the Gospels; and that is well no doubt for the history of Christianity. But what we do find, all shows how deeply the mind of Jesus was imbued with the old prophetic imagery. We read the exquisite words of the Psalm:

xxiii, 1
> The Lord is my shepherd, I shall not want,
> He maketh me to lie down in green pastures,
> He leadeth me beside the still waters.

Is. liii, 6

Or we hear the penitent cry: "All we like sheep have gone astray," and we know how it is that the herald of the kingdom proclaimed that he Mt. xv, 24 came to save "the lost sheep of the house of Mk. vi, 84 Israel," and to gather those who "were as sheep not having a shepherd." The great tenth chapter of John, that plays so intricately on the figure of the good shepherd and the fold, is nothing more than a legitimate interpretation of the Master's sayings in the spirit of prophecy. The parable is clear to us, however it may have puzzled the hearers at the time. Milton was but carrying on the continuous tradition of both Testaments when he mingled the imagery of the pastoral poets with the apocalyptic hopes of heaven:

> Weep no more, woeful shepherds, weep no more,
> For Lycidas your sorrow is not dead,
>   . . . but mounted high,
> Through the dear might of him that walk'd the waves,
> Where other groves, and other streams along,
> With nectar pure his oozy locks he laves,
> And hears the unexpressive nuptial song,
> In the blest kingdoms meek of joy and love.

There entertain him all the saints above,
In solemn troops and sweet societies,
That sing, and singing in their glory move,
And wipe the tears forever from his eyes.[2]

The kingdom announced by Christ, as we try to picture it to ourselves, is not without complications, even apparent contradictions, and may never have been clearly defined in Christ's own mind. Only on one point there was no complication and no uncertainty: however the kingdom itself might be conceived, whether as a pastoral paradise, or as a magical transfiguration here and now of earthly things into celestial glories, or as an otherworldly heaven, it is always the sphere of God's rule, the immediate and unimpeded reign of Jehovah, always a realization of the petition, Thy will be done on earth as it is in heaven. And with insistent urgency the call to men was to repent. God's will would be done, that was certain, however the doing might manifest itself; but to the individual man then living it meant everything whether he was in a state of submission or rebellion to the divine purpose. Only those who put themselves into a proper attitude by penitence for their sins would pass unscathed through the terrible ordeal (the

[2] *Lycidas,* 165 et seqq.

peirasmos, "temptation," as it became in Greek) and enter into the peace of God.

Mk. i, 15 Above all there was needed a liberation from doubt, and the summons to repent is equivalent to a command to have faith: "Repent ye, and believe (*pisteuete,* have faith in) the gospel." Of the relation of faith to Christ's work of healing and other supernatural acts we shall have more to say when we come to discuss the question of miracles in general. Here the point to note is that the faith of repentance meant such an awakening of the soul to its own birthright as would render it the master instead of the slave of physical law. Faith is a living realization, by what may be called the spiritual imagination, of the otherworld everywhere immanent in these opaque bodies of earth. So much is true of all religion. More specifically, repentance unto faith in the mouth of Jesus demanded such a purging of the mind as would prepare the convert for the advent of the kingdom of God: "faith is the substance of (the giving of substance to) things hoped for, the evidence of things not seen." Very soon, at any moment, the heavenly world was to break in visibly upon the present order; God should reveal Himself and no longer hide His omnipotence in the clouds. What now seems

miracle, at the Parusia would be nature, and
only those in whose souls a like transformation
had taken place would be at home in that transfigured world, or could endure its glory.

The expectation of a visible descent of heaven
upon earth, however it might occur, was the form
in which religious faith had become petrified,
one may say, among the Jews, and in which it
presented itself to Jesus. Inevitably the otherworldliness of the gospel proclaimed in Palestine two thousand years ago was involved in a
mythology which belonged to that special time
and that peculiar people; we can see how vividly
the myth dominated the mind of a Paul in the
first generation of the Church. But the kingdom
did not appear; and there is an element of truth
in the theory that the whole inner history of
the Church turns on the procrastination of the
Parusia, and on the effect wrought in the mind
of believers by the continual disappointment of
their hope: the growth of religion has been the
slow "de-eschatologizing" of Christianity.

Meanwhile, in the lands which had not been
held back by a reactionary nationalism such
as had checked the progress of Israel under
the Maccabees, faith was taking other forms.
Through all the various Oriental myths which

had thrust themselves into the Hellenistic world, and not entirely suffocated by the monism of the dominant philosophies, the purer, simpler vision of Plato had held its place. Now what repentance and otherworldliness meant to Plato we know from his wonderful story of the cave. I need not repeat the details of the allegory, but the words in which Socrates gives the key to its imagery are intensely significant for the history of Christianity. "Our argument (*logos*)," he says, "points to this faculty as already in the soul of every man. And it happens thus: as the eye [in the case of the prisoners in the cave] could not turn from darkness to light without the whole body, so that organ with which we perceive the truth must be turned about with the whole soul from the world of generation, until it is able to endure the light of pure being and of the brightest and best of being—that is to say, of the Good. . . . And this is conversion."[3] Now whatever this or that critic may think of the spiritual value of the process, it is a fact that for three centuries the development of Christianity is marked by a slow merging of the eschatological otherworldliness of Jesus with the philosophical otherworldliness of Plato. This

[3] *Republic*, 518 c.

is not the place to follow the steps by which, from
generation to generation, the kingdom of heaven
lost its mythical actuality and became transformed into a name for life in the eternal world
of Ideas. But a single passage from one of the
great Cappadocians of the fourth century may
be cited as evidence of the final result of the
coalescence:

"Blessed, it is said, are the pure in heart, for
they shall see God. Now the kingdom of heaven,
my brothers, you must know is nothing but
the true understanding of things that are (*tôn
ontôn*), which understanding also the Scriptures
call blessedness. For the kingdom of heaven is
within you. And for the inner man we can say
that there exists only contemplation (*theôria*).
The kingdom of heaven then would be contemplation. For the things of which we now behold
as it were the shadows in a mirror, of these things
later, when we have been freed from this earthly
body and have put on an incorruptible and immortal body, we shall see the archetypes. We
shall see them, if we govern our life in the straight
course, and make the right faith our care, without which government and care no one shall see
the Lord. For, it is said, into an evil-doing soul
wisdom shall not enter, nor will it dwell in a
body subject to sin. And let no one object, and
say: Ignoring the things that lie at our feet, you

summon us to a philosophy concerning the incorporeal and altogether immaterial being. For I judge it absurd to permit our senses to fill themselves with their own matters, while the reason (*nous*) alone is prevented from its proper energy. For as sense is capable of attaining what is sensible, so reason is capable of attaining the things of reason (*tôn noêtôn,* the Platonic Ideas)."[4]

St. Basil's conception of the otherworld is more philosophical than Christ's, and presents the kingdom of heaven in language as valid today as it was yesterday. So much one must grant; and I would be the last to belittle the transmuting task of the Church under Greek influence. Nevertheless we must reckon with the fact that the impelling force lies in the words of Jesus himself, and not in those of Basil or any other of the great theologians of the faith; it was Christ and no other that made Christianity. And that is because to him belonged in a supreme degree the gift of spiritual imagination, the divine energy of vision without which all teaching and preaching fail to move the will, and so leave the hearer wondering perhaps but unconverted. For Christ the otherworld was the one absorbing re-

[4] Basil, Letter viii (Migne IV, 265), at the conclusion of a long discourse on the Trinity.

ality, and it could possess this reality for him
and for others only by standing forth in palpable living images. It was so with Plato also, who
created the Ideal philosophy by the poetry of
the *Phaedrus* and the *Symposium*. But there
was needed something more than the poetical
philosophy of Plato to stir the sluggish heart of
the world, and that something was given by
Jesus, the prophet of Nazareth.

How, then, does it stand with us? Shall we
dismiss the actual belief of Jesus as an empty
myth, and, disregarding his words, make our account with the Platonized faith of the Church?
The kingdom of heaven as it was proclaimed in
Galilee can be for us, you will say, only a symbol.
Yes; but it is a symbol of power today and always for the reason that behind it lies the reality
of an everlasting truth. The Parusia was announced by Christ as an imminent event, yet the
manifestation did not come, and has not come,
and, we suppose, never will come. That is the
nature of symbols. Nevertheless the awful fact
abides that the otherworld is about us and in us,
seemingly ever ready to break through the thick
crust of material forms. And however the un-
heeding world goes on, for each living soul death
lurks at the threshold, ever threatening, always

about to come; and death certainly comes. We believe that in death, whether it be in the hour of transition or for an age of time, the veil is rent and things visible and things invisible change places; that for a moment at least the soul is stayed in its flight through the fleeting clouds of illusion, and is made aware of immutable judgement; that for one moment at least a full sense of its responsibility is thrust upon it as by a light flashing from the eternal throne of righteousness; and then perchance it pursues its swift blind way—for a season. Such a truth lies behind the symbolism of Christ's eschatology; though in trying to express the naked reality one falls into other and feebler imagery. The ever-present kingdom is the reverse of the fatal mutability of all terrestrial things:

Passing away, saith the World, passing away.[5]

When Jesus asked the twelve whether they too would go from him, Simon Peter gave the answer, which we may repeat today: "Lord, to whom shall we go? thou hast the words of eternal life."

Jn. vi, 68

[5] Christina Rossetti, *Old and New Year Ditties.*

CHAPTER V

PURITY AND HUMILITY

PRIMARILY repentance is remorse for disobedience to the will of God and a lifting of the mind from present things to faith in the imminent coming of the kingdom of heaven. But repentance implies also such a change of life as would ensue upon the awakening of faith; it is the link between otherworldliness and morality.

Now the eschatological theory has raised a new problem in regard to Christ's ethical teaching. The point is this. If the kingdom is about to break upon the world like a devastating storm, annulling the old relations of man to man and placing all things under the immediate will of Jehovah, what room is left for the practice of the ordinary virtues? Repentance, in such a case, would be the call to prepare one's self for this catastrophic change and to submit to the divine purpose, but it would have no meaning for the conduct of men in a natural state of society.

To meet this difficulty the propounders of the eschatological view have invented an imposing term, *Interimsethik*: life in the kingdom would be "supernormal," "beyond good and evil," and the only ethics Christ taught, they say frankly, was for the brief interim before the grand event, and would have little or no value if that event should fail—as it did fail. In support of their thesis they quote the statement that in the resurrection there shall be neither marriage nor giving in marriage, but men shall live as the angels in heaven.

Well, it may be that Christ thought of existence in the kingdom as angelic, but to describe such a life as beyond good and evil is to introduce a metaphysical distinction which has no place in the New Testament and, I suspect, has no meaning for those who so glibly use the words. The Messianic rule in the imagination of Jesus as in the later Prophets may have been supernatural, it was never supermoral. More than that: any unbiased reading of the record will force the conclusion that, if a comparison must be made, Christ's teaching in regard to the kingdom is relatively obscure and sporadic, whereas his insistence on righteousness is clear and continuous. Instead of a harsh contrast between the

supermorality to come and a provisional behaviour here and now, the distinctive note of the
gospel is rather the puzzling manner in which
the act of repentance with a view to the expected
catastrophe merges into an ethic of universal
otherworldliness for this present life, as if the
great change had already occurred.

If any one passage should be chosen to show
this blending of the temporary and the eternal
at the centre of Christ's ethical teaching, it would
be, I think, these words spoken, according to
the chronology of Mark, just after the rebuke
to Peter for his worldly conception of the Messianic rôle:

"Whosoever will come after me, let him deny   viii, 34
himself, and take up his cross, and follow me.

"For whosoever will save his life shall lose it;
but whosoever shall lose his life for my sake and
the gospel's, the same shall save it.

"For what shall it profit a man, if he shall
gain the whole world, and lose his own soul?

"Or what shall a man give in exchange for his
soul?

"Whosoever therefore shall be ashamed of
me and of my words in this adulterous and sin-
ful generation; of him also shall the Son of man
be ashamed, when he cometh in the glory of his
Father with the holy angels."

Here we have first a plain reference to the actual situation; he who would go with the Master on the perilous journey to Jerusalem must be prepared for hardship and self-denial.[1] That is the force of "after me"; yet in the next verse the similar phrase "for my sake" hints at something in the personal claims of Jesus which, as we shall see later, lifts the gospel high above the level of eschatological warning. So also the last verse brings the vision of an immediate Parusia before the listeners in very concrete imagery; and it is with this event in mind that Jesus summons the disciples to venture their lives. Yet again, in the verse that follows the challenge to make the great venture, the word previously translated "life" is now rendered "soul"—and rightly, for the sense has quite shifted.[2] It is no longer present life weighed against life in the new dispensation, but the baser part of a man against the better part. In Christ's conception of the kingdom the otherworldliness of faith was not perfectly redeemed from the old monism of his race, which failed to discriminate clearly between things visible and things invisible; but the

[1] The word "cross" in the first verse must come from the Church after the crucifixion, but as a whole the passage is certainly authentic.
[2] This, of course, is entirely in accordance with the ambiguity of the Greek word *psyché* and the Hebrew equivalent *nephesh.*

morality implied in his use of the word soul,
though it may have its root in the hope of a be-
atified earth, reaches up to a dualism of universal validity. He would have men balance the desire of the spirit against the desires of the flesh,
and, through all hazards, save that member of
their composite being which, in the language of
St. Basil, knows God and contemplates the
everlasting realities.

Critics have found difficulty in the attitude
of Jesus towards the ethics of the Old Testament, and particularly in the apparent contradictions of the Sermon on the Mount. At one
time he seems to abrogate the Law entirely,
while in other verses he declares that it is eternal, and that not one jot or tittle of it shall fail
until heaven and earth pass away. And after his
departure we know that the early community
was for a time divided in its views of Christ's intention. Yet there ought not to be any real ambiguity here for one who considers the whole
scope of his teaching. It is a case of distinctions,
and I do not remember that the matter has ever
been put more neatly than by one of the Valen-
tinian Gnostics of the second century, in a letter
to a woman who had asked for instruction.[3] In

[3] Ptolemaeus in Epiphanius, I, xxxiii.

the body of the Law, he says, we must first distinguish between what was added by man and what came from God. The former, including the mass of traditional regulations now found in the Pentateuch, Christ abrogated utterly. The second, the veritable law of God, again falls under three heads. One part has to do with the typical, or symbolical, acts of worship, such as Sabbaths and sacrifices; and these rules Christ did not annul, but transformed and spiritualized, changing, for example, the paschal sacrifice into the eucharist. Another part had been enacted as it were in condescension to the weakness of men, and embraces such precepts as "an eye for an eye"; for this he substituted a new law of a different order. The third division, the true voice of God as spoken, for instance, in the Decalogue, is immutable in its nature; and this Christ did not alter, but confirmed and deepened.

Now these distinctions come from a tainted source and may seem scholastic in their formalism; but they do give a fair indication of the varying attitude of Christ towards the Law in the Sermon and elsewhere. It was the burdensome rules of men, and not the written law, he had in mind when he denounced the righteousness of the scribes and Pharisees: "Full well ye

Mk. vii, 9

reject the commandment of God, that ye may
keep your own tradition," and when he exposed their hypocrisy by declaring that what
came out of a man's heart, not what entered into   Mk. vii,
the mouth, brought defilement. Of the law which
professed to come from Jehovah he uttered no
such words. The *lex talionis* he abrogated indeed, yet without indignation, and only by put-
ting in its place other precepts of the Pentateuch more in harmony with the Decalogue. It
was these ordinances of fundamental morality,
summed up in the Ten Commandments, that
Christ pronounced eternal; their validity should
abide when the kingdom was established, no less
than in the dark days of trial, even until heaven
and earth had passed away. In these he found
the two principles of purity and humility which
run through the Beatitudes and are the Christian way of otherworldliness; and these he restated in terms of the new law which is, as it
were, the soul of the old law.

"Thou shalt not commit adultery": so ran the
letter of the Law. Now, not only the unclean act   Mt. v, 28
but the impure thought was to be condemned:
"But I say unto you, That whosoever looketh
on a woman to lust after her hath committed
adultery with her already in his heart." Nothing

would need to be said of this new formulation
of the law, which indeed speaks for itself, were
it not for a philosophy current in these days,
against which it might seem to have been promulgated with prophetic foresight. We hear much
of the dangers of repression, and we are told of
the mischief that comes from checking desires
and preventing them from passing into action.
And, unquestionably, there is an element of
truth in this theory, as in all pernicious theories
that catch the popular mind. It is possibly true
that, under certain conditions, it may more
damage the character, may more loosen the
moral fibre, to nurse unclean thoughts in the
heart than to permit them to wreak themselves
in action. It may be; but, even so, the law of
Moses would be brought into question, not the
law of the gospel, for it was precisely the principle of purity as enforced by Christ that repression should begin in the imagination. And it is
important to add that, generally speaking, the
first step towards controlling the imagination is
to impose an inhibition between the fleeting fan-
cies and their consummation in deed. At any
rate this fact cannot be shaken: between the current philosophy of our day, which in the end,
whatever be its measure of truth, means prac-

tically that each man shall do as he desires, and the Sermon on the Mount a wide gulf is set. Licence lies on one side, the liberty of religion on the other.

But purity touches more than the sins of the flesh, being used, as the grammarians would say, by synecdoche for the opposite of that whole range of desires which fall under the *libido sentiendi.* And especially it includes release from the craving for wealth in all its material forms. When, on the way to Jerusalem, a certain young man kneeled at the feet of Jesus and asked what he should do to inherit eternal life, the first direction was that he should obey the moral precepts of the Decalogue; and then, when the young man professed to have observed all these, the command was added: "One thing thou lackest: go thy way, sell whatsoever thou hast, and give all to the poor, and thou shalt have treasure in heaven." The young man, we are told, went away sorrowful, for he had great possessions; and Jesus, looking round upon his disciples, said: "How hardly shall they that have riches enter into the kingdom of God!" And the disciples "were astonished beyond measure, saying among themselves, Who then can be saved?" We who read the story are apt to regard their

Mk. x, 17

astonishment as naïve: but was it really so? Christ was inculcating no rule of charity as we understand the word, but enforcing the law of the soul against the law of things. And I suspect that, despite the almost universal testimony of philosophy and religion, about the last truth we learn is the deceptive bondage of possessions, the deadening touch of the cares of this world, and the impossibility of serving both God and Mammon.

The purpose and reward of purity are declared in the beatitude, "The pure in heart shall see God," and reinforced in the maxim, "Where your treasure is, there will your heart be also." With Christ the thought was primarily of preparation for life in the new state, when the desires of the flesh should be ended and there should be no more marriage or giving in marriage, and when those who were not fit for the transfigured earth should flee in confusion before the visible face of Jehovah. Again the warning is eschatological; but it is none the less universal for that, and to belittle it as *Interimsethik* is to allow one's self to be hag-ridden by theory. "The light of the body is the eye: if therefore thine eye be single, thy whole body shall be full of light. But if thine eye be evil, the whole body

shall be full of darkness." Plato was saying the
same thing in figures of another sort when he
declared that the soul which has made itself impure with the lust of material pleasures, and has
brought itself to believe only in truth which
exists in corporeal forms such as a man may
touch and see and taste,—that the soul so pol-
luted can have no portion in the radiant beauty
of the Ideal world, nor know those fair desires
that are as wings to carry it above the clouds of
illusion, nor ever come into communion with
the gods.[4] Strip off the metaphorical language,
though by doing so the truth is not so much
purged as deprived of its vital energy, and the
meaning of Jesus and Plato is the same: they
would say that in the workshop of the imagination where the desires are forged the great battle of religion is waged and the question decided
whether a man shall lose his soul or save it. You
may say that we create our own enemies; but,
once created, they are there, and they shall beset us as demons leagued together for our ruin:
"For we wrestle not against flesh and blood,   Eph. vi, 12
but against principalities, against powers,
against the rulers of the darkness of this world."

In comparison with purity the virtue of hu-

[4] *Phaedo*, 81, 82.

mility is a more complex idea and more difficult to comprehend, as also its roots strike more deeply into the ground of religion. In part it too bears the stamp of that provisional ethic to which the upholders of the eschatological view of the kingdom are fain to reduce all the teaching of Christ. So the constantly repeated precepts of self-abasement may have their temporary application. "If any man desire to be first, the same shall be last of all," "whosoever of you will be the chiefest, shall be servant of all,"—such rebukes to apostolic ambition, taken at least at their face value, may seem rather to resemble prudential maxims than laws of morality; for, after all, those who were now to serve should in a little while, almost in the twinkling of an eye, be set upon thrones of glory to judge the twelve tribes and the world. The sons of Mammon have been wise enough to practise humility of that sort. But, again, to stop here would be to prove one's self a slave of one's theory. The inheritance of the earth may have been promised to the poor in spirit, but surely not in order that they might be lifted up in pride.

In its wider scope humility is the contrary of that sin of *aponoia,* spiritual pride, which, even more than the seductions of pleasure, was re-

Mk. ix, 35

Mk. x, 44

garded by Christian theologians as the original
cause of the Fall and the source of evil. And as
spiritual pride has a twin root, in the intellect
and in the imagination, so humility of spirit is
double.

"I thank thee, O Father, Lord of heaven and   Mt. xi, 25,29
earth, because thou hast hid these things from
the wise and prudent, and hast revealed them
unto babes. . . . Learn of me, for I am meek
and lowly in heart." This saying of Jesus, which
belongs to the common source of Matthew and
Luke and is assuredly genuine, became one of
the leading commonplaces of Greek theology.
It was known to St. Paul, and restated by him   I Cor. iii, 18
in the harsh paradoxical language so natural to
his overwrought spirit. It was used by Justin
Martyr and by apologist after apologist in their
contention with the upholders of pagan philosophy. It was admitted by Origen, most erudite
of all the Fathers. Athanasius employed it with
telling effect. Ambrose turned it into a neat epigram: "It has not pleased God to give His people salvation in dialectic."[5] It is current again
today as the guiding idea of one of the dominant, if very questionable, schools of German
theology; and a Harnack, lumping together in

[5] *De Fide*, i, 5: *Non in dialectica complacuit Deo salvum facere
populum suum.*

one sweeping condemnation all those, orthodox
and heretic, who sought to wed Christian faith
to philosophy, will say, "that ethics and religion
do not at all come within the sphere of the intellectual, and that the intellect can produce nothing of religious value."[6] What shall we make
of all this? We may put aside the thesis of
Teutonic liberalism as a gross exaggeration, if
not a distortion, of the truth; yet there are the
words of Christ, and there is the fact that the
wisdom of Greece failed to move the world's
heart, until it bowed in submission to the foolish-
ness of the Cross. Must the Christian say that it
is as hard for the philosopher to enter into the
kingdom of heaven as for the rich man, and that
education as well as worldly possessions is a bar
to religion? Surely not that. But I think we must
admit, in sober sadness, that the intellect too
brings its temptations, that the man who reasons is prone to deceive himself, that science has
a tendency to close the mind in a narrow circle
of self-complacency, and that the professed agnostic is peculiarly liable to a callous conceit.
Such, we know, was the discovery of Socrates
when he set out on his search for the wise man,
and found everywhere, and most prominently

[6] *History of Dogma*, II, 327.

there where reputation for wisdom was greatest, that men thought they knew what they did
not know at all. Thus scepticism became in the
Platonic philosophy the door of access to the
realm of Ideas, just as humility is the virtue by
which the Christian enters into the kingdom of
God.

It is this way. As the desires of the flesh are
the necessary instruments of the material life,
yet in the interest of sanity need to be guided
and checked, so we must recognize the limitations of reason if we would live reasonably. And
just because our guide in practical conduct is
reason, the abuse of reason creates the deepest
disorder in our being: "If therefore the light   Mt. vi, 23
that is in thee be darkness, how great is that
darkness!" The danger always is that the reasoning man should begin to regard reason as
mistress instead of servant of that within him
which lies deeper than any namable faculty, and
so, in pursuit of the simplifying process demanded by reason, should come to question the
irrational fact of dualism which we accept in the
simplicity of faith and only relearn by the profound searching of self-knowledge. Under the
pride of intellect too often the morality and
otherworldliness of religion shrivel away, leav-

ing its victim spiritually deserted in a waste monotony of his own creation.

Of that form of the vice we shall have more to say when we come to deal with the presumptions of a metaphysical theology. For the present we have before us the naïver vice of the "wise and knowing" Jews who had obscured the inner sense of good and evil by a rationalized interpretation of the Law, and who by pride had closed their minds to the nearness of God and the vision of His coming kingdom. It was in rebuke of the scribes and Pharisees that Jesus uttered his jubilant thanks. It was in the same spirit that he spoke the beautiful words of benediction:

Mk. x, 14, 16   "Suffer the little children to come unto me, and forbid them not: for of such is the kingdom of God.

"And he took them up in his arms, put his hands upon them, and blessed them."

Much has been written to expound what Jesus meant by this tenderest of all the beatitudes, and he who has read the interpreters will probably feel—as I certainly feel—that some things are best understood by leaving them unexplained. Nevertheless, so much one can say: whatever else Jesus may have had in mind, however he may have been moved by love of what is instinc-

tively innocent in humanity, his reference to the
kingdom was made to teach the plain yet difficult truth that unless a man shall preserve to the
end something of a child's wonder at the mystery of the world, he has closed upon himself the
door to spiritual communion. Humility of the
imagination is as necessary to religion as a right
reasonableness. To a child the earth is a place
of play, peopled with creatures of his fancy;
Christ would have us retain that faculty in our
maturer years, only with the conviction that
spiritual things, though hidden to the eyes of
the body, are no vain make-believe, but do veritably speak to the soul in sundry manners. Something of the same sort Plato intended in that
curious passage of the *Laws* (803 c) where he
declares that men fail to make the right distinction between what is serious and what is not.
God, he says, is the natural object of a man's
most earnest and blessed endeavours; yet men
are the puppets of the gods, and in turn our
worship is like the sport of children; we must
go through life as it were a kind of pastime, with
sacrifice and song to propitiate the secret powers.
Not war and ambition, but play is the real business of human existence. In like vein wrote
Thomas Traherne in the seventeenth century,

when for a moment it seemed as though Platonism and Christianity might be finally reconciled of their differences:

"The corn was orient and immortal wheat, which never should be reaped, nor was ever sown. I thought it had stood from everlasting to everlasting. The dust and stones of the street were as precious as gold: the gates were at first the end of the world. . . . Eternity was manifest in the Light of Day, and something infinite behind everything appeared: which talked with my expectation and moved my desire. . . . The skies were mine, and so were the sun and moon and stars, and all the World was mine; and I the only spectator and enjoyer of it. . . . So that with much ado I was corrupted, and made to learn the dirty devices of this world. Which now I unlearn, and become, as it were, a little child again that I may enter into the kingdom of God."[7]

Wonder is the beginning of religion and, as Plato knew, of philosophy, and, so long as that humility is retained, the intellect may go on its inquisitive way with no danger of desiccating the soul. It was Christ's purpose to lay the basis of the spiritual life, not to raise the superstructure, but I think he would not have cavilled at St. Paul's reaching out after the deeper wisdom of

[7] *Meditations*, iii, 8.

experience: "When I was a child, I spake as a
child, I understood as a child; but when I became a man, I put away childish things." Nor
was there any incompatibility between Plato's
principle of wonder and his pursuit of the maturer fruits of reflection, or any discord with
Aristotle's foundation of philosophy on the universal desire of knowledge.[8] Against all the
pride of reason and imagination the beatitude
still holds good: "Blessed are the poor in spirit,
for theirs is the kingdom of heaven."[9]

But there is a humility before man as well as
before God and the mysteries of the world, a
humility that is equally the fruit of self-knowledge. The relation between the two aspects of
the virtue may be seen in the petition of the
Lord's Prayer, "Forgive us our trespasses as
we forgive those who trespass against us," and

[8] Plato, *Theaetetus*, 155 D; Aristotle, *Metaphysics*, I, i, 1.
[9] There has been a good deal of discussion as to whether Matthew's "poor in spirit" or Luke's "poor" represents the actual
language of Christ. Matthew's phrase is equivalent to the "meek
and lowly in heart" of xi, 29; Luke means the "afflicted by
poverty." I suspect they are both right. In the twenty-fifth
Psalm the same root, *'anavim, 'ani*, is translated in the ninth
verse "meek" and in the sixteenth verse "afflicted"; and properly.
The word occurs frequently in the Old Testament with this
double sense, and its full force would seem to be "those who pass
through the want and afflictions of life in a spirit of humble
resignation." The same word belongs to the Aramaic spoken by
Christ; it is found, for instance, in the Targum of this twenty-
fifth Psalm. If then Christ gave his blessing to the *'anavim*, he
would have meant both the "poor in spirit," "meek," and the
"poor," "afflicted."

Mt. vii, 1

in the equivalent command, "Judge not that ye be not judged." Many times as these sayings are repeated, one wonders how often their full meaning is grasped, or any realization comes to the mind of the scope and devastating sway of the vice of censoriousness. Self-knowledge of any kind is hard to acquire, a slow and often a bitter lesson; but of all forms perhaps the hardest, and in its acquisition the bitterest, is the very simple truth that we are as other men, that our trespasses, the faults of our disposition and the errors of our mind and the wrong-doing of our hands, are like the trespasses of other men, that we have no special warrant or immunity from the universe. Theoretically every man knows this well enough, but practically and in his heart of hearts! I suspect indeed that no man feels the force of that truth who has not first learnt the meaning of humility before God.

In conduct the virtue of humility finds ex-
Lk. vi, 31
pression in the Golden Rule: "As ye would that men should do to you, do ye also to them likewise." In the Sermon on the Mount, where the
Mt. vii, 12
same precept is given, the clause follows: "For this is the law and the prophets"—and it might be added, not of Israel only but of the world. Hillel and Philo knew the Rule in slightly dif-

ferent form, thus: "What is hateful to thee, do
not to thy neighbour." It was taught by Con-
fucius in far-away China: "What you do not
want done to yourself, do not do to others."[10] It
was a familiar proverb of the Hindus:

> One law there is: no deed perform
> To others that to thee were harm;
> And this is all, all laws beside
> With circumstances alter or abide.[11]

The same rule was current among the Stoics
and is found elsewhere in classical literature. It
might, without forcing the note, be taken as a
formula for the comprehensive virtue of justice
opposed to the vice of covetousness (*pleonexia,*
the desire to overreach one's neighbour in any
field) and to that instinctive self-love (*philau-
tia*) which sets one's self in a different plane
from other persons, and is nothing but an acute
form of self-ignorance. In this sense, as the
enemy of covetousness and self-love, humility
may be called the meeting-ground of Christian
and Platonic ethics:

"Oh men, we shall say to them, God, as the ancient report is, holding the beginning and the
end and the middle of all things that are, moves
straight on to His goal by the seemingly devious

---

[10] *Analects,* xv, 23.
[11] Böhtlingk, *Indische Sprüche,* 3253.

ways of nature, and with Him follows always Justice, the avenger of those that depart from the divine law. To this Justice he that will be happy clings, and follows with her, humble and chastened."[12]

[12] *Laws*, 715 E. See *The Religion of Plato*, 262, 276.

CHAPTER VI

THE GREAT COMMANDMENT

IT will have been observed that the parallels and probable sources of the Golden Rule agree in this, that they are all negative, whereas the formula of Christ is positive. Now superficially considered it may seem to make little difference whether you say, Do not unto others as you would not have others do unto you, or, Do unto others as you would have others do unto you; but in that shift from the negative to the positive there does enter something new, an emotional content that connects the Golden Rule with the more distinctive Christian rule of love.

"Thou shalt love the Lord thy God with all thy heart, and with all thy soul, and with all thy mind. Mt. xxii.

"This is the first and great commandment.

"And the second is like unto it, Thou shalt love thy neighbour as thyself.

"On these two commandments hang all the law and the prophets."

It must be admitted that, as the record of the gospel stands, the law of love does not occupy the signal place commonly accorded to it in our thought, and is in fact much less insisted on than the more specific virtues of purity and humility; yet at an early date the Great Commandment was lifted out of its casual context and set in the centre of Christ's teaching. To Paul love was greater than faith and hope; in the first epistle of John what in the gospel was the essence of the Law becomes the heart of theology: "God is love, and he that dwelleth in love dwelleth in God and God in him." And so the Church came to believe that in the Great Commandment it had a possession which marked it off from the world.

Love as the motive power behind purity and humility is the essence of Christian ethics; there can be no question of that. But love is a term of many meanings, ambiguous in any language, particularly so with us of English speech, which has only one hard-worked word to express what was distinguished in Greek by three or four quite different words. What exactly was signified by love in the mouth of Jesus?

The question cannot be shirked, yet I confess I take it up with reluctance. There are terms

that resemble the witch's apple of the fairy tale,
clean and single to the eye, but on one side bearing a deadly poison for the unwary taster. And
love is one of these. Any reader acquainted with
the Christian literature of edification knows that,
as a rule, the more volubly the principle of love
is advocated, the more surely will the book be
filled with mawkish sentiment and pious inani-
ties and false ideas of life. It should seem almost
as though the exaltation of love measured the
degradation of religion. A virile mind is likely
to acquire a kind of disgust for the very sound
of the word; yet there it lies, at the heart of the
gospel, we must do the best we can with it, and
above all try to obtain a clear comprehension of
its meaning. Perhaps the safest approach to such
an understanding will be through certain exclusions and distinctions.

In the first place, then, Christian love signifies something more than the bare altruism of
charity, in the diminished sense of the word.[1]
We need to recall the order of the two rules that
constitute the Commandment. Apart from the
flood of books which are contracting religion to
a mere branch of Sociology, no one can hear

[1] It is a pity that the word "charity" should have been degraded
from the sense of Christian love in general, as the equivalent of
St. Paul's *agapē;* but so it is.

many sermons today without being struck by the strong humanitarian trend which lays all the emphasis on service to our fellow men and slurs over, when it does not utterly ignore, the obligation of love to God. And as a consequence no one can fail to note a tendency to think more and more of the material well-being of others—not to mention of ourselves—and ever less of their spiritual needs. If we turn from the pulpit to the dustier ways of philology we can see the change of interest curiously reflected in the history of one of our common English words. "Comfort ye, comfort ye my people, saith your God," was the command of Jehovah to His prophet, and that is the meaning we are wont today to read into the Great Commandment—but with how different a consolation! Think of what was conveyed by the word comfort in the phrase of the Prayer Book: "The most comfortable Sacrament of the Body and Blood of Christ, . . . whereby we are made partakers of the Kingdom of heaven"; or of what the translators of the Bible had in mind when they chose this word for Paul's salutation: "The God of all comfort, who comforteth us in all our tribulation, that we may be able to comfort them which are in any trouble." So it was in the older

Is. xl, 1

II Cor. i, ᵇ

secular literature. When, for instance, Sir Per-
civale and Sir Bors met with Sir Galahad in the
wandering quest of the Sangreal, this is how Sir
Bors greeted his friend: "Hit is more than yere
and an half, that I ne lay ten tymes where
men dwelled, but in wylde forestes and in mountains, but God was ever my comforte."[2] And
when John Winthrop left his home to sail over
the sea to America, this was his farewell: "I shall
parte from thee with sorrowe enough; be comfortable my most sweet wife, for God will be
with thee." And again, a little later in the same
century, one of the minor poets was writing:

> When shall my soul receive
> A comfortable smile to cherish it,
> When thou art gone?[3]

But now what has the word, one of the most
precious heirlooms of our speech, become to us?
Plumbing and butcher's meat and an easy bed.
And these are good things; but surely religion
desires something more. It is no exaggeration
to say that in the altered meaning of that familiar word comfort we can measure a long
lapse from the peace and joy we were commanded to share one with another in the love of
God.

[2] *Morte Darthur*, xvii, 19.
[3] William Chamberlayne, *Pharonnida*, II, v, 362 et seqq.

I do not forget Christ's own denunciation of those who called on his name, yet neglected to feed the hungry; nor St. James's definition of pure religion and undefiled; nor St. John's protest: "He that loveth not his brother whom he hath seen, how shall he love God whom he hath not seen?" And all this is true, just as we have seen at every turn that there can be no sound religion without morality. But this is the point: the otherworldliness of religion, or, more precisely, the desire of the soul that lends peremptory reality to the otherworld, is expressed in the first clause of the Great Commandment, while the morality of religion, or at least the social aspect of morality, enters with the second clause; and to separate the love of man from the love of God is simply to betray religion with a kiss—in the end it may prove a very dubious ethics. Certainly in the gospel the stress lies overwhelmingly on the element of otherworldliness: "Seek ye first the kingdom of God and *His* righteousness." Having that fact in mind, we shall see nothing inconsistent with the charity of the Sermon on the Mount when Christ declares to those who would enter upon the path of religion that the love of father or mother must yield to love of their guide upon the way, or, as the same truth is expressed more paradoxically by Luke, that the disciple must hate his father and mother, his wife and children, his brothers and sisters.

And, secondly, Christian love does not sanctify the love of the flesh. It might appear superfluous to argue so obvious a fact, but such is very far from being the case. History shows only too clearly that there is a hideously deceptive similarity between the two kinds of emotion, and that there is a constant tendency in religious excitement to seek relief in physical indulgence. The orgiastic rites of pagan antiquity are notorious, and the corruption that at an early date crept into the so-called Christian love-feasts can be matched by happenings today. The danger is persistent and universal. Indeed, however we may read with abhorrence the accounts of temple worship tolerated among highly civilized peoples of the past, probably no age was ever more liable than our own to the insidious confusion of the celestial and the carnal loves. Our literature draws much of its nourishment from this confusion, sometimes dressing out the earthly love (which may be fair and honest enough in its own place) with the brightest hues of heaven, sometimes, and increasingly today, greeting the satyrs of the jungle as if they were champions of human liberty. How should it be otherwise when the dominant philosophy and psychology of our schools profess that inhibition is unwholesome and that a man's first obligation is to develop his individual temperament? We need to be delivered from cant in these things, and to repeat to ourselves that the love of the Great Commandment is profoundly diverse from the *libido sentiendi*.

And we need to be saved from pedantry also; one would like to say that we need to be delivered from Kant as well as from cant. You will read much in the German theologians about the eudaemonism of St. Paul (and, by an inevitable extension, of Christ himself) as compared with the Categorical Imperative of Kant, and you will meet frequently with the assertion that the ethics of the New Testament must be restated for the modern man in the terms of the Kantian absolutes, or, if that cannot be done, must be relegated to a low stage of moral development by the touchstone of our more advanced spirituality. Now that I say boldly is pure pedantry, or something worse. I say, with all the conviction of which I am capable, with whatever of authority long years of reading and reflection may warrant,—I say, looking forward to other matters we shall have to discuss, that the German conceit of what Kant accomplished in philosophy and of what Luther accomplished in religion, this conceit that fairly leaps at you out of the pages of German theology and that has hypnotized modern scholars, is one of the great barriers in the way of philosophical and spiritual truth. I am not minimizing the results of German research, on which indeed I am making heavy draughts in the writing of this book; but I am asserting that the Kantian metaphysic spells death to philosophy, and that the Lutheran theology spells death to religion.

The Categorical Imperative, which severs the moral sense from the desire of happiness and declares that we must do our duty with no thought of the consequences to ourselves, is the emptiest of metaphysics, meaningless at the best, fraught with a base cargo of hypocrisies at the worst. Schiller's parody of the Kantian theory is apt:

Willingly serve I my friends, but, alas, with glad inclination;
So I am tortured to know whether I'm moral at all.[4]

[4] *Die Philosophen.*—In the *Bhagavad Gîtâ* the rule is given that man should do his appointed work without attachment and with no thought of the results, but not without thought of achieving the happiness of liberation. In the right sense of the word Hindu religion is as eudaemonistic as Platonism or Christianity. See *Hellenistic Philosophies*, 127 et seqq.

So too the Kantian dictum that in all our conduct we must think of each act as if we were to formulate a law for the universe, is a caricature of the Golden Rule,—again, a meaningless presumption at the best, and at the worst an excuse for intolerant fanaticism. I understand what Christ meant when he bade me treat my neighbour as I would have him treat me; I tremble at the inferences that might be drawn from Kant's identification of my acts with a universal law.

The mischief arises from the false assumptions of reason; and I hold it a fact that no moralist would object to the simple postulates of religion who had not first argued himself out of his innate consciousness of dualism, or somehow lost his sense of the radical distinction between happiness and pleasure. No man who possesses a vivid realization of otherworldliness, whether it take the form of Plato's Ideas or of Christ's kingdom of God, will be afraid of eudaemonism. The whole doctrine of salvation in the Platonic philosophy implies a self-love as the last and finest motive of conduct, though Plato knew also of a self-love that lies at the source of utter ignorance and evil. In a like manner, however profoundly we interpret the Christian law of love, there is not a word in the gospel to support the notion that love of God and of one's neighbour excludes or supplants the love of self that comes with true self-knowledge. The Great Commandment brings us back to the text which we took as the keynote to Christian ethics. Jesus said that he who would save his life should lose it, but he added immediately: "For what shall it profit a man, if he shall gain the whole world, and lose his own soul? Or what shall a man give in exchange for his soul?" Nothing. In the ethics of Christ there is involved a thoroughgoing dualism; the gospel is a message of joyous eudaemonism.

Further, the law of love, as it is not metaphysical, so is not sentimental. You will find nothing easy-going in the preaching of Christ, but a strenuous appeal to character. The word is always: "Enter ye in at the strait gate, for wide is Mt. vii, 13 the gate and broad is the way that leadeth to destruction." For no other class of men did Christ show such contempt as for the weak and shifting and undecided, for those who put their hand to the plough and then turned back. He never trifled with human nature. He proclaimed a religion of the will, rather than of sentiment, and it was easy for later theologians to attach to the gospel a theory of evil as having its roots in indolence and effeminate slackness. Charity may be long-suffering and slow to wrath, but it does not inculcate an indiscriminate condoning of baseness and evil. Jesus dismissed the woman taken in adultery without condemnation; but he added significantly: "Sin no more." Neither does charity lend any countenance to the maxim that we should hate sin but love the sinner; for how, indeed, shall you discriminate between the evil-doer and his evil, unless you regard evil superficially as a kind of garment which can be put on and off rather than as a quality of the soul itself? It is true that many passages of the Gospel might seem to imply that Christ showed a preference for sinners over the outwardly righteous; but we must remember that Christ saw—and the Church has followed him in its doctrine of spiritual pride—that self-righteousness deadens the conscience and leaves a man almost without hope. It is the inner lie of Plato, the complacent illusion of knowledge against which no argument prevails. Infinite compassion may be the note of the Gospels, and the life of Christ was spent for the salvation of sinners; but he never forgot the call to repentance, and in the end he could condemn without reprieve. As for the daemonic rulers of this world, who

Jn. viii, 11

were so to speak the personification of evil, one
remembers his exultant cry: "I beheld Satan as Lk. x, 18
lightning fall from heaven."

The love of the Great Commandment is not
mere altruism; neither is it sexual love, nor a
metaphysical abstraction, nor easy-goingness,
nor indiscriminate compassion and readiness to
forgive. So much for exclusions and differences.
If you ask, then, what it *is,* I should say that at
the last we do not know what anything *is,* but
that so far as we can trace its operation it seems
to be associated with the imagination positively,
as humility was associated with it negatively; or,
in other words, it reveals itself as the active principle animating that virtue. The humble man,
in the religious sense, is he who sets a check upon
the tendency of the imagination to magnify his
personal importance above that of other persons, or to visualize himself, so to speak, as a
reality in the world to the overshadowing of
other selves. Love, as we define it, would be that
outreaching power of the imagination by which
we grasp and make real to ourselves the being
of others.

That might appear to be a faculty universally
possessed and easily exercised; but to any effective degree it is not so. To begin, as does the

Commandment, with God, we may talk fluently about a divinity within the world, but actually to realize the being of a Divine Person, to be conscious of His presence in such a way that our emotions and will are affected as they are by thinking of a human friend, to rise above the pallid reverence of Deism, or to believe in anything more individual than a "power not ourselves that makes for righteousness" (and it is well if we can do that), to be able to lift the soul into the warm communion of prayer and worship,—ah, that does not come by taking thought or by the wisdom of the schools or by virtue of the marketplace; it is the rare gift of the spiritual imagination. Newman was right when he averred that the one supreme difficulty of faith was the belief in God, and that, with this possession, all else in religion was easy. Really to believe in God—for such a boon a man might be ready almost to give his soul in exchange. If Christianity has any meaning, it means that the knowledge of God culminating in love was bought for us at the price of the Incarnation.

It will be said that, however difficult it may be to conceive the existence of God, no such obstacle confronts us in regard to human personalities; and this to a certain degree is true. Only

a brain crazed by metaphysical scruples enter-
tains any doubt about the existence of other persons. Nevertheless, to realize another person
in his full rights, to get out of one's self, so to
speak, and into him, to comprehend the peculiar
complex of inheritance and environment that
form the background out of which his character
emerges,—that is not at all easy and is very far
from common. Hence the force of the precept,
Judge not that ye be not judged. The wrong
done is not in judging others, but in judging
them unimaginatively, without comprehension.
Legally suc'ı judgement may be necessary, since
the law can scarcely go beyond the cognizance
of facts; but individually and religiously we
need a more elastic criterion, and there is nothing
incompatible with justice in hanging a man and
at the same time offering priestly consolation.
Yet, even so, it does not follow that the religious
precept against judging implies any relaxation
of the moral law or any compromise with evil.
Plato was anticipating Christian doctrine when,
in the *Gorgias,* he contended that, if all punishment is for the sake of purging and correcting
the soul, then a wise man conscious of guilt would
voluntarily offer himself to trial, and *would
treat a friend in the same way.* Only let him be

Jn. xvii, 21

sure that he proceeds from particular knowledge, and not, like the young Euthyphro in the dialogue of that name, from the presumption of a hasty generalization. The love that inspires the Golden Rule demands that a man should first look closely into his own soul and its springs of good and evil. Christ himself did not refrain from condemning, and condemning harshly; but he also displayed an extraordinary accuracy in seeing into the secret heart of others, and it is by virtue of this faculty that we think of him as coming to judge the quick and the dead.

It may be objected that this faculty of the imagination still falls short of love, and that we may have a full realization of other persons without that desire for their well-being which the Great Commandment requires. I doubt if in practice such a severance can be made, but I admit that something else besides knowledge enters into the act of imagination, a feeling which nowhere perhaps has been stated better than in the words of Jonathan Edwards:

"That consent, agreement, or union of Being to Being, . . . viz., the union or propensity of *minds* to mental or spiritual existence, may be called the highest, and first, or primary beauty that is to be found among things that exist:

being the proper and peculiar beauty of spiritual and moral Beings, which are the highest and first part of the universal system for whose sake all the rest has existence. Yet there is another inferior, secondary beauty, which is some image of this, and which is not peculiar to spiritual Beings, but is found even in inanimate things; which consists in a material consent and agreement of different things in form, manner, quantity, and visible end or design; called by the various names of regularity, order, uniformity, symmetry, proportion, harmony, etc. . . .

"Probably it is with regard to this image or resemblance, which secondary beauty has of true spiritual beauty, that God has so constituted nature, that the presenting of this inferior beauty, especially in those kinds of it which have the greatest resemblance of the primary beauty, as the harmony of sounds, and the beauties of nature, have a tendency to assist those whose hearts are under the influence of a truly virtuous temper, to dispose them to the exercises of divine love, and enliven in them a sense of spiritual beauty."[5]

That is to say: as in perceiving the consonance of inanimate objects we are thrilled by an aesthetic pleasure, so from the consent of soul to soul we derive a kindred but profounder happiness; and as he who has felt the pleasure of

[5] *The Nature of True Virtue,* chap. iii.

physical beauty desires to multiply the sources of that pleasure, so he who has felt the purer happiness will labour to increase the spiritual harmony from which it flows. To the Platonist the consent of soul to soul springs from the mutual perception of the eternal and immutable world of Ideas; on that sympathy of interest depends the strength of friendship and the social unity of the State. With Christianity the emphasis shifts from the perception of Ideas to the knowledge of God; as St. Basil says, "by community of faith men are led to spiritual union."[6] From the joy rising out of his own consent to the being of God the Christian will reach forth to other human souls, and strive after fellowship with them in spiritual happiness; "That they all may be one; as thou, Father, art in me, and I in thee, that they also may be one in us: that the world may believe that thou hast sent me."

Jn. xvii, 21

Does this consent of being to being, this benevolence of faith, precede the imaginative realization of other persons, or does it follow? Which is cause and which effect? I suspect that in the end such a question is idle and that the two cannot be separated, any more than we can make a

---

[6] Letter cliv Migne. This thought is a commonplace among the Fathers.

final divorce between will and knowledge. In the secret workshop of our nature it may be that some obscure act of volition is the decisive factor in that intimate partnership—such would seem to be the lesson drawn from a comparison of Christianity and Hellenic philosophy—but as we approach the matter from the surface and in the imperfection of practice I believe that the stress rightly falls upon the need of comprehension.

CHAPTER VII

AUTHORITY

At the close of Christ's Sermon on the Mount it is said that "the people were astonished at his doctrine, for he taught them as one having authority"; and that note of authority is perhaps the final impression left by a study of the Gospels, as it opens the profoundest and most difficult question of interpretation. On what did it rest? You will discover nothing original in his proclamation of the kingdom or, as far as we can see, in his notion of the kingdom; the old idea that he converted the popular hope of an earthly triumph of Israel to the reign of God within the heart has been exploded by better knowledge of the eschatological literature. Nor was there anything to startle his hearers in the call to repent or in the morality of repentance. Purity and humility had formed the very warp and woof of prophecy, and the commandment of love is borrowed literally from the Law itself. So also his spiritualization of the Law, the trans-

ference from outer observance to the inner intention of the heart, may have been in contrast
to the prevailing method of the scribes and
Pharisees, but this too had been anticipated in
Scripture. "I the Lord search the heart," is the
word of Jehovah to Jeremiah, "I try the reins, xvii, 10
even to give every man according to his ways,
and according to the fruit of his doings"; and
the same thought runs through other prophets
and the Psalms.

For reasons easily understood pious scholars
have sought to magnify the originality in the
substance of Christ's doctrine, and have been
loath to admit the scope of his dependence on
the Old Testament. Sometimes the attempt
grows desperate. "Almost all Christ's moral
precepts," we read in one such commentator,
"might be paralleled or illustrated by something
in Hebrew or Jewish literature. This praise of
the beauty of flowers cannot, apparently, be so
paralleled. And it helps Christians to approxi-
mate to a realization of the spiritual altitude of
Christ's conception of beauty and glory in the
moral world."[1] As for beauty in general, Dr.
Abbott must have forgotten the line in his morning anthem, which strikes, I think, the keynote

[1] E. A. Abbott, *The Son of Man*, 714.

Ps. xcvi, 9   to the Book of Common Prayer: "O worship the Lord in the beauty of holiness." And if the last phrase, taken from Coverdale's translation, is a loose generalization for the specific direction, "in the holy ornament prescribed for the Temple," it is in harmony, nevertheless, with the whole spirit of the Psalter. As for flowers, not to mention the Song of Solomon, the hopeful parts of prophecy are radiant with the idyllic charms of nature; the kingdom appears regularly to Isaiah and his compeers as a renewal of earth's loveliness in the Garden of Eden.[2] No, the striking fact is the extraordinary degree to which the mind of Christ was steeped in the thoughts and imagery of the canonical Scripture, and this, to a nearer view, marks the strength, and not the weakness, of the religion he established.

So far as there is originality in the ethics of Jesus it must be sought rather in the form than in the substance of his doctrine. His genius, though he wrote nothing, was that of a great literary artist; if it were not for the sound of the thing, one might say that he was the master rhetorician of religion. And this literary, or rhe-

[2] It is not irrelevant to cite from the Mishna the prayer of R. Jehuda, to be pronounced at sight of the flowering of spring: "Blessed be He, who letteth nothing fail in His world, who hath created fair creatures and fair trees that men may rejoice therein."

torical, gift might be more narrowly defined as
a unique power of condensation and pithy utterance. We do not know the character of his longer
discourses, how he held the multitudes spell-
bound for hours until they fainted with hunger;
we think we would give the bulk of many librar-
ies to have the record of what is lost forever.
Time has deprived us of much, yet it has saved
for us what, after all, must have been the strength
of his appeal,—those memorable sentences which
he tore out of the very heart of truth, bringing
together what was dispersed, giving a new turn
to what was ineffective, packing into a maxim
what had been left more or less to inference. It
was such a flash of insight that gave a positive
turn to the Golden Rule, and that combined a
saying in Deuteronomy with another in Leviti- vi, 5
cus to form the Great Commandment.[3] It was xix, 18
genius of a like sort that collected petitions scattered through Hebrew literature into the incom-
parable prayer which expressed the immediate
longings of the disciples for the visible kingdom
of God, yet could satisfy the deepest spirit of
worship through all the ages. It was as a poet of

[3] This union of the two loves is found in the *Test. of the XII
Patr.* (e.g., Iss. v, 2; vii, 6; Dan v, 3), and is regarded by Dr.
ᴗharles as an anticipation of the gospel. Probably, however,
Kautzsch is correct in holding the book in its present form as the
work of a Christian writer.

words that he summed up the love of natural
beauty in one perfect image: "Consider the
lilies of the field, how they grow; they toil not,
neither do they spin: and yet I say unto you,
that even Solomon in all his glory was not ar-
rayed like one of these." Further than that the
seeing eye has not gone. And so of his use of
parables, his revelation of human sympathy in
dealing with the woman of Samaria or with the
woman taken in adultery, his resource of defen-
sive epigram in replying to the questions about
tribute to Caesar and his own authority,—there
is nothing comparable to these in the memoirs
of Socrates or in the sacred books of Buddhism;
"never man spake like this man."

It must be remembered, too, that the record
of Christ's talk is not only tantalizingly frag-
mentary, but has been transmitted to us through
a peculiarly unsuited medium. Classical Greek
at its best has marvellous resources, but of all
languages its idiom is most foreign to that of
the Hebrew or Aramaic; and the Greek of the
Evangelists is an impoverished dialect, most
inadequate when, as in Luke, it tries to be most
literary. We of the English speech are fortun-
ate in that, owing to the character of our tongue
and to the fact that the makers of the Author-

Mt. vi, 28

Jn. vii, 46

ized Version were steeped in Hebrew, our Bible
probably brings us closer to the gravity of
Christ's teaching than the original Greek. In-
dividuality of style rather than any invention
of new matter gives the personal stamp to
Christ's teaching. When higher criticism has
done its best, or its worst, this note will remain
untouched as sufficient proof that in the Gospels we hear the authentic voice of one who
lived and preached in Galilee.

If then the teaching of Jesus is in substance
little more than a continuation of the Old Testament, what authority has it for us of today, to
whom the voice of prophecy comes muffled by
the long passage of time? Christ's doctrine of
the kingdom was ephemeral, and maintains its
value only as a vivid symbol of the otherworldliness of all religion; what of his morality? In
the view of the thoroughgoing eschatologists his
call to repentance carried with it only an *Interimsethik,* suitable for the brief interval of waiting. Such a theory, as I have tried to show, quite
misses the point. No, if we feel anything impracticable in the precepts of Christianity, that
is not because of their temporary character, or
of the special form in which the otherworld presented itself to Christ's imagination; it is rather

because the purity of his religious attitude tends to overshadow the workaday concerns of life.

We must recognize the fact, and adjust ourselves thereto as best we can, that there are two phases of morality: the humanistic, represented in pagan literature by Aristotle, and the strictly religious, for which Plato is the great philosophical spokesman of antiquity.[4] Now humanism is the way of the world and of humanity caught in the web of ever-changing needs;

> *Immortalia ne speres monet annus et almum*
> *Quae rapit hora diem.*[5]

Its law is the Golden Mean, the balance between extremes, expounded in the *Nicomachean Ethics,* and its ideal is that honesty which seeks as its reward a fair share of earthly pleasures for a life of wise activity.

Such a compromise was not in the mind of Christ, as it never is with the masters of religion. A good deal of nonsense, I fear, has been talked about the Golden Rule and the Great Commandment, as if they gave a simple and practicable solution of the problems of life. I think a clear-headed Christian will admit that, taken

[4] For a broad discussion of this distinction between the two planes of life I may refer to Irving Babbitt's *Rousseau and Romanticism, passim.*
[5] Horace, *Odes,* IV, vii.

literally as Jesus intended them to be taken, they cannot be applied to the complexities of society, and that he who should really love God with all his heart and his neighbour *as himself* would find it difficult to adjust his conduct to the exigencies of an artificial civilization. But it by no means follows that the ethics of pure religion is hypocritical or valueless or even secondary.

The difficulty of humanism, with its law of the Golden Mean, is to determine what shall be reckoned fair and wise, and to settle the true point of moderation in the sliding scale between two vicious extremes: to decide, for example, just where decency lies between ascetic purity and ugly licence, where self-respect descends to humiliation and where it rises into empty pride, what are the boundaries of a permissible self-love; and in that ever urgent dilemma a true humanism will temper the insistent desires of nature, and correct the tendency to pursue the easier downward course, by keeping one eye, as the saying is, upon the supernatural heights. That is the explanation of Aristotle's tenth book which appends the doctrine of divine contemplation rather awkwardly to the preceding discussion of practical conduct.

Perhaps we can get a clearer notion of the relation of the two spheres of morality by taking one of the specific virtues. At the extreme of humility lies the principle of non-resistance, which has been the subject of endless controversy. To turn the other cheek, to repulse no borrower, to hand over one's cloak when one's coat has been snatched away, are not practical precepts for a civilization based on property and dependent on the police court; yet there can be no doubt that Jesus meant his words to be understood quite literally. His thought was not on the compromises of a worldly life. At the other extreme lies the law of violence, the reign of the prince of this world, as Paul called it, which bids a man grasp at what he can, and makes might the criterion of right. And this too is antisocial and impracticable; it would reduce society to a state lower than that of a pack of wolves.

Plainly the humanist will endeavour to mediate between these two extremes; but just where in the scale of compromise shall he take his stand, saying, thus far will I go and no further? At the lowest he will see that the indiscriminate use of violence is inhuman, and will stop at the law of retaliation, demanding an eye for an eye, a tooth for a tooth. But he will soon discover

that the *lex talionis,* though carried out with the
strictest equity, tends to increase the amount of
violence in the world and needs to be tempered
by approximation to the religious law of non-
resistance. Again the question is: how far shall
he go in this mitigation of natural justice?

There is no fixed point of compromise, no
definite law of mediation; yet upon compromise
and mediation rests the very possibility of a
moral humanism. In that uncertainty the important matter for all men, for the humanist or
the religious, is to know where he stands and
what he is aiming at. If he would be a man of the
world, as most of us must be, let him measure
his place honestly, admitting to himself that the
perfect righteousness of the otherworld is not
for him here and now, striving always to rise to
the plane that lies just above him, making no
compromise with the truth however he compromises in his daily conduct. On the other hand,
if he would be a saint, let him understand the
consequences of his choice, and abide by them.
It is not without reason that the ancient Church,
perceiving what Christ meant by non-resistance,
made martyrdom the final test of faith; and
martyrdom today may come in other ways than
death—in the loss of property, the surrender of

honours, isolation from the common pursuits and ambitions of men. I cannot help feeling that the guardians of the Church today as a whole fell into lamentable error during the recent war. There is no such thing as a religious war, it is a frank appeal to the law of violence; it may be necessary in a world of compromises, but it should be recognized as such, and the attempt to throw the glamour of religion over its horrors is to bring the planes of morality into utter confusion. We might have been spared the humiliation of seeing two hostile peoples each praying to the same God for the ruin of the other.

This earth would be a sorry place were it not for the few men always in it, who, while living among the things of time, have their hearts set wholly on the things of eternity. We whose life must be regulated by the shifting law of humanism, have need of the saints. Take out of the world Plato and Jesus, and the slender line of their faithful disciples, and what would our western civilization be? Newman, I am bound to think, in his defection to Rome made something like the great refusal; yet take Newman out of nineteenth-century Oxford and all we of the English speech would be impoverished to a degree of which we are perhaps not duly conscious. So closely knit is the organization of society, so much of our best we possess by a kind of vicarious participation in the lives of those who are strong and know. It is the thought of their liberty that supplies a place of refuge and refreshment for the imagination of those who at times must fret under the bondage of compromise. And today, one suspects, the number is larger than it was yesterday of those who have doubts about the final validity of our civilization and feel certain uneasy qualms over the multiplication of mechanical devices for the uplifting of society; what would it not mean to them if they heard the clear, sober, unhesitating voice of one man proclaiming the ancient truth?—

"Lift up your eyes to the heavens, and look upon the earth beneath: for the heavens shall vanish away like smoke, and the earth shall wax old like a garment, and they that dwell therein shall die in like manner: but my salvation shall be for ever, and my righteousness shall not be abolished." Is. li, 6

"What shall it profit a man, if he shall gain the whole world, and lose his own soul?" Mk. viii, 36

Because we hear in the words of Jesus this unaltering truth of religion, pronounced without compromise, expressed with the power of arresting conviction,—for this reason, if for no other, they sound today with the same authority as two thousand years ago. But that is not all. He was a teacher of righteousness and other-worldliness, yet, as we shall see, claimed to be something more; and by that something more he converted religion into Christianity.

CHAPTER VIII

THE MESSIANIC SECRET

SUCH was the gospel of the kingdom preached by Jesus. For his hearers the message was, Repent and prepare yourselves for the great and terrible event; for us the burning question is what he thought of himself in relation to the kingdom and how he spoke of himself to the people. On one point all the records agree, that in his own thoughts he was the Messiah of prophecy; and unless that fact is accepted as authentic, we may as well give up all attempts to deal with his life historically. But in regard to the revelation of himself the records differ. In Mark he reveals himself privately to the apostles but nowhere announces his mission publicly until the trial scene; whereas in the other two Synoptics—and increasingly in the order of composition—the secret is less carefully kept, and in John is not kept at all. Now in general Mark has come to be recognized almost universally as the oldest and most accurate account of the actual events, and in this particular matter it is easy to see how Mark's reticence might have been misunderstood or forgotten by the later writers, but hard to see how the reverse should have occurred. We may then begin with the view that Jesus announced the kingdom openly and appeared as a prophet of repentance, but exercised a certain reserve as to his personal mission.

And this concealment is altogether natural. Consider what a frank proclamation of himself as the Messiah would have entailed. A prophet —though until the appearance of John no clear prophetic voice had been heard for many years —yet made no extraordinary demand on the Jewish faith. But with the Messiah it was different. We may suppose that the more extravagant theories of the apocalyptic books had not obtained much hold upon the populace, whose instruction came from hearing the canonical Scriptures in the synagogues; nevertheless the simpler conception of an earthly king from the line of David had been largely overlaid by the hope of a miraculous deliverer who should suddenly be revealed in all the manifest glories of Jehovah. At any rate this was the belief of Jesus himself. How then should he, a man walking

about in the flesh, known to be the son of a carpenter in Nazareth, even though his Davidic
birth were admitted, pose as the expected Saviour? Naturally, in his present state such pretensions must be veiled in obscure hints, if they
were indicated at all.

It was owing to the stress of this difficulty,
apparently, that he adopted the peculiar title
of Son of man, which is never used in the synoptic Gospels *of* Christ, but seems to have been
his regular designation for himself in his more
solemn utterances. Now, as we have seen, this
phrase, the Son of man, is curiously ambiguous.
On the one hand, in accordance with Semitic
idiom, it signifies no more than "man," "a particular man"; yet at the same time it was employed by Daniel as a mystic name for the glorified people of Israel, and in the eschatological
literature it had come to be one of the terms for
the Messiah, the Son of God. The phrase was
thus suited admirably to the ambiguity of Jesus'
position and perhaps to the lingering uncertainty in his own mind. It is not to be expected that
the documents should preserve the niceties in
his use of the appellation, but one may gather
from Mark that he employed it differently to
serve the time and occasion. When, for instance,

Mk. ii, 27

the Pharisees rebuked him for allowing the disciples to pluck the ears of corn on the Sabbath, he excused the act on the ground that "the Sabbath was made for man, and not man for the Sabbath"; and then he added: "Therefore the Son of man is Lord also of the Sabbath." Is "Son of man" here merely a repetition of the generic "man" that precedes, or does it refer to Christ himself? Critics differ in their interpretation; to me it seems that the ambiguity was designed, and that Jesus was speaking at once of man in general and of himself as something more than man. On other occasions the appellation pointed unmistakably to the Messiah, but was so cast into the future that it might or might not be applied to the speaker. In this way he did not commit himself; and at the same time his language corresponded with his actual position, for though in one sense he was now the Son of man, in another sense the title, as equivalent to the Messiah, would belong to him only when the great event had occurred and God had exalted him to be Lord of the kingdom. In private among his disciples he appears to have employed the title less cautiously, yet even there in such a manner as to arouse rather than to satisfy their curiosity, until the hour of revelation struck.

On the whole this view of the Messianic secrecy seems to offer the best key to the synoptic narrative, though it must be admitted that we touch here on several highly debatable problems. Why on various occasions when the demons recognized him as the Holy One of God, or the Son of God, did he rebuke them, and forbid them to make him known? Now this matter of demonic possession takes us into a province strange and, one must say, uncomfortable to the modern intelligence. But, however we may feel, it would be nothing unusual that to Jesus and his companions the phenomena of mania should be caused by devils who had their habitation in the souls of men, and that these spirits should have an intuition of things spiritual not granted to mortal eyes. What actually happened, why these demoniacs trembled before Jesus and cried out for mercy, may remain shrouded in mystery; but of the fact of the command to keep silence, there can scarcely be a doubt. Perhaps, as it has been suggested,[1] Jesus was unwilling to have his mission announced through unclean channels;

[1] Eduard Meyer, *Ursprung und Anfänge des Christentums*, I, 103.

more probably, I think, he shrank from a premature revelation of any kind. The time was not yet come.

His frequent charge to those whom he healed of other, less malign ailments raises a question of a different sort. Why, it is asked, should he have sought to impose silence in cases where, as often happened, the miracle was performed in the presence of a crowd and concealment was impossible? And what shall be said of the strange and sporadic reserve in his teaching? After the parable of the sower and the seed it is reported that the Twelve in private questioned him, and were told that to them it was given to know the mystery of the kingdom of heaven, whereas to the multitude all things were hidden in parables, in order "that seeing they may see and not perceive, and hearing they may hear and not understand; lest at any time they should be converted, and their sins should be forgiven them." What can be the meaning of this mystification in regard to a parable containing nothing which might not be proclaimed from the housetop? or what sense could there be in preaching repentance in language deliberately designed to prevent understanding? Something has gone wrong with the record, that is plain.

Mk. iv, 10

To the sceptically inclined these inconsistencies have offered a handle for attacking the veracity of the whole narrative. They hold that Jesus never for a moment thought of himself or acted as the Messiah and had no occasion for concealment or mystification, that the Gospel of Mark (which is the source of the misunderstanding) was written when the Church, influenced by the supposed Resurrection, had transformed him into a supernatural figure, but while men were still alive who remembered having got no such notion of him from his actual deeds and words. Hence, these critics argue, the secrecy about miracles and the esoteric teaching would represent a clumsy attempt to cover over the transition from the memory of Jesus as an ordinary man to the conception of him as a wonderworker and inspired prophet.[2] I confess that the logic of this argument is too subtle for me, as indeed most of the reasoning of the liberal and semi-sceptical school seems harder to accept than the difficulties it undertakes to explain. I suspect rather that the secrecy in regard to the miracles is a confused and misplaced tradition of times when he did seek to escape notoriety; for it is clear enough that his mission often

[2] This is the theory set forth by W. Wrede in *Das Messiasgeheimnis in den Evangelien.*

weighed upon him as an almost intolerable burden. As for the puzzling reserve in his teaching and the failure to comprehend his plain statements, these too may very well be a misapplied recollection of an embarrassment that must have confronted him at times in his public ministry.

On one occasion we can see him extricating himself from such an embarrassment in a manner which throws light on the whole situation. John, who had announced the coming of Elias[3] as the herald of the kingdom, was now confined at Machaerus by Herod. Possibly he may have had some premonition at the time of the baptism that Jesus was the expected prophet. At any rate he was naturally stirred by the rumours of great events taking place in Galilee, and sent messengers to inquire whether this was he who should come or whether they should look for another. What should Jesus reply? He could not speak the truth fully and openly. He might have sent back a bare denial, but that again he could not honestly do. He might have proclaimed himself the prophet Elias who was to precede the Messiah, and whom John expected;

Mt. xi, 2

[3] This is the view of the thoroughgoing eschatologists, and I let it stand here for what it is worth. The documents are not clear on this point, nor is it essential to our thesis. Certainly Jesus regarded John as the forerunner and himself as the Messiah.

such an admission would not have excited indignation, for the people were ready to acknowledge him as a prophet; but that would have been to falsify his real Messianic claims. As it was he took refuge in a more or less transparent evasion. "Go and show John again," he said, "these things which ye do hear and see; the blind receive their sight, and the lame walk, the lepers are cleansed, and the deaf hear, the dead are raised up, and the poor have the gospel preached to them." It was left to John to recall the words of Isaiah prophesying the advent of the Messiah:

> Then shall the eyes of the blind be opened,   Is. xxxv, 5
> And the ears of the deaf shall be unstopped;
> Then shall the lame leap as an hart,
> And the tongue of the dumb shout with joy.
>
> .   .   .   .   .   .
>
> He hath sent me to bring glad tidings to the humble,   lxi, 1
> To bind up the broken-hearted.

Or John might refer the miracles to Elias, who, according to the prophecy at the end of the Old   Mal. iv, 5
Testament, was to appear as the forerunner of   Is. xl, 3
the great day, and to prepare the way for God's anointed. And then, when the messengers had gone, Jesus turns to the bystanders and, moved perhaps by the solemnity of the event to reveal more of his secret than he had done before,

breaks into that superb eulogy of John, declaring that John himself was the Elias he looked for, with the inference, for those who had ears to hear that he, Jesus, was the Christ.

According to the account of Matthew the messengers from John came just after Jesus had sent out the disciples in couples to disseminate the gospel, whereas Mark and Luke connect the mission with Herod's inquiry whether Jesus were not John come to life again. Unfortunately the whole story of this missionary enterprise, which must have been one of the cardinal points of Christ's life, is so entangled in other events, and in Matthew at least so coloured by the later experiences of the Church, that it requires something like a surgical operation to lift it out of its context. The Twelve, or, as Luke says in one of his reports, the seventy, were sent out at a time of tense expectation, when the harvest seemed ripe for the reapers, and the fatal moment was not only near but actually at hand. So much would appear to be certain. The missioners were charged to sound a warning through the towns of Galilee, taking nothing with them to provide for the journey. As a warrant for their authority they were to heal the sick and cast out devils. They were to meet with insults and opposition, to pass through fire and sword, and Satan himself should be leagued with evil men against them. These things were the necessary prelude to the day of Jehovah, as had been foretold by all the prophets, a part of the Messianic woes, and even before the emissaries had gone over the cities of Israel the Son of man would appear and the powers of darkness should be overwhelmed. It all reads as if Christ, in sending out his disciples, expected never to see them again, never, at least, in this human unchanged state. Yet they did return, reporting indeed great victories over the devils, but beyond that nothing; there were no signs of the world's uprising, no indications of the breaking day. It is not easy from the narrative to tell how Jesus was affected by this surprise, or disappointment. We have on the one hand his exultant cry, "I beheld Satan as lightning fall from heaven," and the words of the "jubilation." And on the other hand, side by side with this note of triumph, stands the bitter curse of Capernaum and the other towns, whose fate in the day of judgement shall be more intolerable than that of Sodom. Which is right, the joy or the wrath? Possibly both, the jubilance over the disciples' manifestation of power, the disappointment that withal the world remained just as it had been. Certainly Jesus was stirred to the depths of his soul by the mingled success and failure of the mission.

v, 32
In Mark the story continues that when the disciples had returned to him, and made their report, "they departed into a distant place by ship privately." Again the record is miserably confused; but so much would seem to be clear, that a change occurred in the nature of Christ's ministry and that more and more he sought to be alone with his friends. It was now, apparently, that he left the region of the Galilean lake with the little band and went north into the heathen country about Caesarea Philippi and Mt. Hermon. What was the cause of this flight, as it may be called? Had the people assumed a new attitude of distrust towards him, as the older commentators were wont to infer? In fact there is no evidence at all of waning popularity, and the same throngs pressed about him in his later Galilean days as in his earlier. Did he go away to hide himself from Herod and so avoid the calamity that had overtaken John? This may have been a contributory cause, for, according Lk. xiii, 31 to one account, Jesus received a plain warning that Herod was plotting to kill him. But it

THE MESSIANIC SECRET 155

should appear from his contemptuous message to "that fox," that the threat did not much alarm him. The cause is rather to be sought in a deep disheartening of Jesus at the course of events. The populace flocked to him as before, they brought their sick to be cured, no doubt they exhibited great curiosity at his preaching and were swayed by his eloquence; but beyond that they could not be moved. They listened, and applauded, and then, all but a few, went away each to his own business. Earth was deaf, the heavens also were obdurate. Could it be that God for some reason was not yet appeased? That He waited upon that wave of true repentance which no amount of warning could arouse? Or, perhaps, did the fault lie with the preacher himself, and was something expected of him that he had not yet fulfilled?

Whatever the cause may have been, the interlude of retirement between the public ministry in Galilee and the journey to Jerusalem must be regarded rather as a voluntary withdrawing of Jesus than as a desertion of him by the people. The two great events of the period are the confession of Peter and the Transfiguration. All three of the Synoptics relate the events in this order, Mark and Matthew noting an inter-

val of six days between them, Luke for some
reason changing the time to eight days. This is
one of the very few precise statements of chronology in the record, and should not be lightly set
aside; yet good arguments have been adduced
for inverting the sequence and placing the Transfiguration before the confession. Some time soon
after the return of the missionaries, if we accept
this rearrangement, and somewhere in the neighbourhood of the Galilean Lake, Jesus went up
into a mountain to pray, taking with him Peter
and James and John. He would be alone with
his nearest associates, where in the solitude of
the hills he might commune with his own spirit
and with God; in this hour of perplexity he
would seek guidance, as he had done on the first
day of his ministry. As for the disciples, we may
suppose that the excitement of the expedition,
with its triumphs over the diabolic powers, was
still fresh in their minds, and their wonder may
have been further aroused by the jubilant utterance and authoritative denunciations of Jesus.
Who was he, their Master, who seemed to hold
in his hands the key of the kingdom, who spoke
of God as no other man durst, whose mortal
eyes discerned the flaming downfall of Satan,
and to whom the vision of the ruin of the un-

heeding cities was open? In such a mood they
beheld his countenance and his raiment transfigured with a white shining light, while Moses
and Elias, personifying the Law and prophecy,
talked with him, and out of an overshadowing
cloud came a voice, saying, "This is my beloved
Son, hear him." It is idle to inquire into the
exact nature of what happened, or to apply the
prosaic instrument of psychology to its interpretation; still more futile to dismiss it as pure
fiction. When we know so little, why strive to
be overwise? For those who hold to the eschatological theory, the significance of the scene lies
in the conversation as the four came down from
the mountain. For the three chosen disciples
there could be no more concealment; they knew
that he with whom they walked was no other
than the very Christ. What they said, what
words of adoration escaped them, we are not
told; but we know that Jesus commanded them
to keep the secret strictly. Only one thing
troubled them: how was it that the scribes, in
accordance with prophecy, looked first for the
coming of Elias, yet Elias had not appeared?
And Jesus, in the allusive indirect manner which
seems to have been habitual with him, replied
that Elias had indeed come, and was rejected,

and had suffered the last indignity. "Then the disciples understood that he spake unto them of John the Baptist."

If we accept the proposed transposition of events, it was with this revelation in the memory of the favoured disciples that the retreat into the North took place. Somewhere in the Hellenized country about Caesarea Philippi—perhaps, as imagination fondly pictures it, near the red limestone cliff from which a source of the Jordan bubbles down—Jesus put the question to the little band of followers, composed probably of the twelve apostles: "Whom do men say that I am?" And the answer came, expressing no doubt the uncertainty of the speakers as well as the current opinions, that to some he was one of the prophets, to others Elias, or John the Baptist come again to life. Then followed the searching query: "But whom say ye that I am?" It should appear that up to this hour the three who had been with him on the day of the Transfiguration had kept the secret, and only now the impulsive Peter, thinking perhaps that Jesus was withdrawing the embargo of silence, spoke out the fateful words: "Thou art the Christ." How the disciples took the revelation, we do not know; there is nothing to suggest that they doubted or

demurred. According to Mark Jesus "charged
them that they should tell no man of him," using
the term of implied rebuke so often put into his
mouth when he enjoined silence. In Matthew,
however, the revelation calls out a blessing upon
Simon, with the extraordinary statement: "And   xvi, 18
I say also unto thee, That thou art Peter, and
upon this rock I will build my church; and the
gates of hell shall not prevail against it."[4]

Whether we follow Mark in placing the confession before the Transfiguration or invert the
order, is no great matter. The important point
to note is that these two events, with the missionary enterprise, form the *peripeteia* of the
gospel drama; the end is now in sight, and we
conjecture that it will be tragic and bloody.
From that time Jesus set his face towards Jerusalem, and began to show his disciples how he
must suffer many things and be put to death.
Peter, we are told, took him aside and rebuked

---

[4] From an early date the rock (*petra*) was identified with Peter
(*Petros*), and it is commonly admitted now by scholars that the
Roman church is right in adhering to this interpretation. The
only valid argument on the other side is the word "this," in the
phrase "on this rock," which would be more naturally referred
to something other than Peter whom Jesus is addressing. The
authenticity of the passage is another matter. I can see no good
ground for questioning it. The word *ekklêsia*, translated "church,"
may well signify the community of the faithful who were to be
taken into the kingdom. The passage has the genuine eschatological ring, and indicates some special authority bestowed on
Peter for the expected season of trial.

him, vowing that these things should not be, as though his own faith were stronger than the Master's. To Christ these words must have sounded like a strange echo of the temptation in the wilderness to escape the burden of his mission, and his reply to Peter was the same as that which he had used at the earlier trial: "Get thee behind me, Satan"; for, as he added, "thou savourest not the things that be of God, but those that be of men." Then turning to the rest of the disciples, he uttered those memorable and enigmatic precepts about the losing and saving of one's life, which we have taken to be the central theme of his moral teaching, though their immediate application is plainly to the attitude of the disciples in the impending crisis. "For the Son of man shall come in the glory of his Father with his angels; and then he shall reward every man according to his works. Verily I say unto you, There be some standing here, which shall not taste of death, till they see the Son of man coming in his kingdom."

Two things stand out in the record of the journey to Jerusalem: Christ's consciousness of the calamity impending upon himself, and the curious inability of his hearers to comprehend perfectly clear statements of what was to happen.

Mt. xvi, 28

Mt. xvi, 27

There are problems here which must be faced
and to which the most diverse answers have been
given. To begin with, it must be remembered in
estimating the significance of Jesus' appropria-
tion of the Messianic woes to himself that in all
the canonical and apocalyptic literature of the
Jews there had been no hint of a defeated and
suffering Messiah; always he was visualized
with the might and majesty of Jehovah about
him, and as the hope of a saviour had receded
more and more from the rise of an earthly monarch to the mystery of a celestial apparition, the
insignia of his office became more incompatible
with human weakness. How had Jesus arrived
at his profoundly original idea, and what support did he find for it in Scripture?

As for Scriptural authority, something occurred here—though in an opposite direction—
like the apocalyptic assimilation to Messianic
prophecy of Daniel's vision of Israel glorified as
the Son of man and appearing before the Ancient
of Days. In those later chapters that constitute
the so-called Deutero-Isaiah there is a beautiful
and haunting picture of the "Servant of Jehovah." In some passages the image clearly represents the people of Israel, now downcast and
suffering, but through their very humiliation

Is. xliii, 2, 10 and obedience to be raised up in glory: "When
Is. xlix, 3 thou passest through the waters, I will be with
thee; and through the rivers, they shall not over-
flow thee. . . . Ye are my witnesses, saith the
Lord, and my servant whom I have chosen. . . .
Thou art my servant, O Israel, in whom I shall
be glorified." Yet mingled with these passages
are others where the imagery cannot belong to
the people, but to an individual man. So, for
instance, immediately upon this address to Israel as the servant of Jehovah and without any
warning of change, come the words:

Is. xlix, 5 "And now, saith the Lord that formed me
from the womb to be his servant, to bring Jacob
again to him, . . . It is too slight a thing that
thou shouldest be my servant to raise up the
tribes of Jacob, and to restore the preserved of
Israel; I will also give thee for a light to the gentiles, that my salvation may reach unto the end
of the earth."

Now it is not hard to follow the process of
personification by which a symbol for the people of Israel becomes transferred to an individual who bears upon himself the destiny of the
nation; nor have we any difficulty in seeing how,
in the case of the Danielic vision, the kingly
Son of man should have been identified with

the Messiah. Likewise, in these passages of the
Deutero-Isaiah, we can understand after a fashion the wavering of the imagery between the
people and the representative of the people.
But, so far as we know, the image of the servant
had never been associated with the Messiah, as
indeed such a connexion required a complete
revolution in the Messianic scheme. We are told
that, in the early missionary days of the Church
Philip found the Ethiopian eunuch reading the
fifty-third chapter of Isaiah and puzzled to know
of whom the prophet spoke: "Then Philip
opened his mouth, and began at the same scripture, and preached unto him Jesus."

Acts viii, 30

If, as seems indubitable, this identification of
the suffering servant of Jehovah with the Son
of man goes back to Jesus himself, how and
when did the belief come to him? We can of
course only conjecture; but in all likelihood it
grew out of the same experience that led to his
retirement and journey to Jerusalem. Consider
the situation. He had gone about the towns of
Galilee predicting disaster and judgement, the
vengeance of God smiting with fire and sword,
and these things had not come to pass; did it
mean that the Messianic woes were to be concentrated first upon himself, and that he, as the

representative of the nation, must undergo humiliation, perhaps even death, as the price of the kingdom? He had summoned men to repentance, and they had listened without understanding; could it be that in some mysterious manner the punishment of the people was to be laid upon him, and that their lukewarmness must be burnt away in the fires of his contrition? Was he designed to be the scapegoat for their sins, and was the spectacle of his shame necessary to draw men to God, as his words had so signally failed to do?

Is. liii, 5

He was wounded for our transgressions,
He was bruised for our iniquities;
The chastisement of our peace was upon him,
And with his stripes we are healed.

All we like sheep have gone astray,
We have turned every one to his own way;
And the Lord laid on him
The iniquity of us all.

He was afflicted yet opened not his mouth;
As a lamb brought to the slaughter,
And as a sheep before her shearers is dumb,
So he opened not his mouth.

.   .   .   .   .

He shall see of the travail of his soul,
And shall be satisfied;

> By his innocence shall many be made innocent,
> For my servant shall bear their guilt.
> Therefore will I give him a portion among the
>   great,
> And with the strong he shall divide the spoil.

With some such thoughts as these, we must suppose, Jesus turned his face towards Jerusalem, determined to put the matter to the test: "He that loveth his life shall lose it, and he that hateth his life in this world shall keep it unto life eternal."[5] Of the bitterness of the final desolation he had some foretaste in the loneliness of the way; he could not make his disciples understand. His first effort to warn them and to elicit their sympathy succeeded only in bringing upon him Peter's rebuke. And again in Mark it is reported: "He taught his disciples, and said unto them, The Son of man is delivered into the hands of men, and they shall kill him; and after that he is killed, he shall rise the third day. But they understood not that saying, and were afraid to ask him." It has been a question among the critics why the disciples failed to comprehend what seems to have been a perfectly plain

ix, 31

---

[5] This is the form of the saying in the fourth Gospel, where it stands in close connexion with the equivalent for the scene in Gethsemane (xii, 27): "Now is my soul troubled; and what shall I say? Father save me from this hour: but for this cause came I unto this hour." I believe that here the evangelist is using material left by the Apostle John.

statement of the future facts, and as usual the difficulty of explaining the text has led to a rejection of the whole narrative as without any historical foundation. Yet it should not be so hard to see what really happened. As the record stands, it is no doubt coloured by an *ex post facto* knowledge of details; whereas at the time Jesus may have had a strong foreboding of trials and dangers confronting him, but no clear foresight of the actual events. It may even be that, though the prospect of defeat had been faced and accepted, yet he still cherished a hope that before that cup was drained to the bottom God would intervene and send down his rescuing angels. The disciples did not comprehend because Jesus himself did not know; only a statement of the precise facts could have convinced them, against their ingrained prejudice, that the Son of man, God's elect regent, was to undergo the indignities which Jesus conveyed to them in vague hints. So they understood not and were afraid to ask. It was a strange and tragic procession that, to avoid Samaria, passed over to the other side of the Jordan, and so Mt. xxiii, 37 wound slowly down to Jerusalem and the cross, —to the city that had slain the prophets and stoned those who were sent to her.

Yet withal the visible signs were anything but
tragic; on the contrary this was in all outward
manifestations the most triumphant period of
Jesus' life, and I confess that to me the contrast between his inner anxiety and his manner
of acting presents the most puzzling problem of
the whole narrative. Evidently the throng at-
tending him on the way were looking for victory
of a very material and palpable sort. This is
made clear by their behaviour at Jericho, when
the blind beggar Bartimaeus cries out to the
son of David for mercy; it assumes the propor-
tions of an incipient revolution at the entry into
Jerusalem; and so far as one can see, Jesus
accepts the demonstrations with entire com-
placency. How shall we reconcile this with his
private warnings? It is easy to say that Jesus
himself was expecting an immediate triumph
and that the forebodings were interpolated in
the story after the event; but in that case we
ought to eliminate also the references to his
commands of secrecy. And that will not do. The
forebodings and the secrecy are not incidental,
they are genuine if anything in Mark is so, and
cannot be torn out of the context. In the crucial
case of the triumphant entry into Jerusalem I
suspect that the explanation of the apparent in-

consistency lies in the fact that we read more into the story than is really there, and that the people did not acclaim him as the Messiah, but as Elias or another whose coming gave promise of a greater to follow. If that be so, Jesus might with perfect consistency encourage the proclamation of the kingdom, while knowing that before the fulfilment of these hopes he himself must undergo the wrath of God. It is at least

xii, 13

notable that, while in the fourth Gospel Jesus is hailed without equivocation as "the King of Israel," the Messianic expression fades away as we trace it back to the earliest form of the rec-

xix, 38

ord. In Luke the salutation is somewhat less precise: "Blessed be the King that cometh in the name of the Lord; peace in heaven and

xxi, 9

glory in the highest." In Matthew the royal title is only implied: "Hosanna to the son of David, blessed is he that cometh in the name of the Lord, Hosanna in the highest"; and, as

xi

Mark reports the words, it is possible to separate the eulogy of Jesus from the glorification of the kingdom: "Hosanna, blessed is he that cometh in the name of the Lord; blessed be the kingdom of our father David, that cometh in the name of the Lord; Hosanna in the highest."* The inference is by no means violent that Jesus was really acclaimed not as the Messiah but as a prophet who was heralding the Messianic time. Matthew supports this theory by his statement that to the inquirers within the city the jubilant crowd called him simply "Jesus the prophet of Nazareth of Galilee"; and certainly Jesus himself, until his final admission to the High Priest, never once during these few days in Jerusalem made an open claim to the Messianic title. xxi, 11

However we interpret the events of the journey and the entry, there can be no doubt that Jesus was soon aware that the last act was tragedy. It should even seem that, short of proclaiming the secret to which he clung with holy reticence, he went out of his way to provoke the authorities and to hasten the end. On their part they appear to have been kept back at first by the fear of incensing the people, and then by want of a definite sustainable accusation worthy

* Dalman (*Die Worte Jesu*, 180) shows pretty conclusively on linguistic grounds that the authentic exclamation is limited to the words: "Hosanna, blessed is he that cometh in the name of Jehovah." There would be nothing necessarily Messianic in such a cry.

of death. If, as seems likely, the betrayal of Judas consisted not in indicating where Jesus might be taken (for such information could have been obtained easily through spies), but in revealing to the High Priests the secret of Jesus' Messianic pretensions since Peter's confession known to the Twelve, we can understand quite clearly what happened at the trial. Various charges were brought, but could not be substantiated by trustworthy witnesses; and to these Jesus answered nothing. Then as a last resource the High Priest put all to the test by the direct question: "Art thou the Christ, the Son of the Blessed?" And Jesus made his confession: "I am; and ye shall see the Son of man sitting on the right hand of power, and coming in the clouds of heaven." Nothing more was asked; nothing more was needed.

I have had no intention to retell these last events of Jesus' life, least of all to offer any obtrusive comments on the agony in the garden of Gethsemane, and the consummation on Calvary. As often as I have read these chapters in all my years from early childhood, I cannot now approach them without being moved to the innermost. Here humanity touches the lowest depth and the highest exaltation. Who was he that in the hour of death forgot the desertion of his disciples, forgot his hopes and transient victories, but not his divine claims: "My God, why hast thou forsaken me!" He knew then the full meaning of our mortal lot, as otherwise he could not have known it, and, knowing that, died in amazement.

CHAPTER IX

SAINT PAUL

I MUST admit that I approach this stage of my study with misgiving and reluctance. Despite the depth of St. Paul's religious experience and the heroism of his life, there are elements in his character which distinctly repel me. Egotism is a trait curiously common in the great reformers who have imposed their beliefs on other men, and one of the nicest problems of religious psychology would be to determine the relation of this trait to the self-denying devotion to truth with which it is often so perplexingly united. But in Paul, along with his readiness to spend his very soul for the salvation of others, there runs a vein of irritable self-assertion which, to me at least, renders many parts of his epistles painful reading.

And then there is the historical question. I cannot but feel that in one way historians have exaggerated the work and influence of Paul, owing to the fact that in Acts and in his own epistles we have a pretty full account of his ministry, whereas for the activities of Peter and the others no such documents exist. Paul represents himself as the great, divinely appointed, and almost exclusive apostle to the gentiles, and Biblical scholars have generally taken him pretty much at his word. Yet it is certain that Paul did not begin the ministry to the gentiles, and that in no sense was he the author of Christianity as a world-religion. For the most part the churches established by him remained comparatively obscure, whereas he had no hand at all, or at best played a very secondary rôle, in the conversion of the three great cities—Antioch, Alexandria, and Rome—which became leading centres of Christian doctrine and discipline. Another of the influential communities, Ephesus, where he laboured for three years, held John chiefly in veneration. So in his dispute with the "Judaizers" and the "pillars" at Jerusalem we have only Paul's version of the story. No doubt he did good and necessary work in hastening the liberation of the Church from the shackles of Hebrew custom; but, again, when we consider his restless vanity, his quick resentment of any intrusion into his field, and when we recall Peter's work at Joppa and Caesarea, we may well ask whether all the liberality was on Paul's side. It is clear, I think, that Peter, possibly the founder, certainly the recognized patron, of the Roman church, must share with Paul the appellation of apostle to the gentiles. In the Gospel of Mark, probably based on Peter's preaching in Rome, we have, with the Logia of Matthew (and perhaps the Logia of John imbedded in the fourth Gospel), one of the two, or three, supremely important documents of our faith; and the main source of our knowledge of Christ is in Mark. The Catholic tradition is perfectly correct: "Thou art Peter, and upon this rock I will found my church."

All this I hold to be true. Yet in another way, in the matter of certain theological dogmas which came into prominence long after Paul's death, we are in danger in the opposite direction of underestimating his influence. The curious fact here is that the Roman church, which otherwise clings so proudly to the Petrine authority, should have fallen so strongly under the doctrinal domination of Paul.

Whatever our attitude towards Paul may be in the end, no one can read the epistles without feeling that, along with, or despite, his egotism, he was sincerely and profoundly religious. And if we look for the roots of his religion in his temperament we shall find them in an intense consciousness of the transitoriness of all earthly things. "The fashion of this world passeth away" I Cor. vii, 31 —that with him was not a mere commonplace or a polite acquiescence in the inevitable, but a terrible and bitter and insistent fact. And the end of all things transitory is death. Transience and death, these are the laws of time, the lords of this earth, and against them every fibre of his being revolted; amidst them he longed, as few men ever have longed, for permanence and life. His writings are permeated from beginning to end with what may be called a horror of death, of that dark abyss into which all things transitory are rushing, and with a desperate hope of life. There is no saying in all his works that opens a deeper insight into his nature than these words to the church at Corinth:

"For our light affliction, which is but for a II Cor. iv, 17 moment, worketh for us a far more exceeding and eternal weight of glory;

"While we look not at the things which are seen, but at the things which are not seen; for the things which are seen are temporal, but the things which are not seen are eternal."

With this haunting sense of the contrast between transience and permanence, death and life, went an equally vivid consciousness of sin and holiness. Like death he abhorred sin, and as life so his desire was set on holiness. There is nothing peculiar in this except the intensity of his feeling, for it may be said that the abhorrence of death and sin balanced against the passion for life and holiness is of the essence of religion at all times and all places. But Paul was a child of his age in the way in which the two threads of the material and the moral are wound together. At one moment the material evil of death and the moral evil of sin are clearly distinguished, while at another time they blend together in one abhorrent idea of corruption; and so of the material and moral blessings of life and holiness, which merge together in the conception of glory.[1] Between these two extremes, corruption and glory, the whole religion of Paul revolves, and his hope of salvation is to escape from the one and to obtain the other.

So far the religion of Paul belonged to the current of Hellenism that had taken possession of the finer spirits of the world in these waning

[1] The word "corruption," *phthora*, combines clearly the double death of body and soul. "Glory," *doxa*, has various shades of meaning in Paul, but in the main it signified, when applied to man, the splendour, the visible light, of the eternal life of the sanctified; it is, so to speak, the manifestation of the spirit, a more vivid expression for incorruption, *aphtharsia.*

days of paganism. It was a faith born of the
union of Greek philosophy and Oriental religi-
osity, and it found an outlet in the various mystery cults which promised a translation from the
corruption of this world into a glorified life
with the gods. But Paul was the scion of a peculiar people as well as a man of his age; he was,
as he himself boasts, a Hebrew of the Hebrews,
of the strictest sect of the Pharisees, brought up
in Jerusalem at the feet of Gamaliel. The virus
of the Rabbis ran in his blood, and, for all his
earnest adherence to Christianity, coloured his
ideas to the end. Perhaps, when all is said, the
radical difference between the teaching of Jesus
and the teaching of Paul will be found just in
this, that, whereas the mind of Jesus was steeped
in the canonical prophets of Scripture, Paul's
mind had taken its bent from the rabbinical
speculations of the age. They affected his eschatology, they are responsible for his theology.

For Paul the opposition of corruption and
glory unfolded itself in a great secular drama.
The world as it came from the hand of Jehovah
was good—that was a belief to which every Jew
clung and which the Christians carried over—
but in its composition, from what source no theologian could say, there was a latent impulse to

Phil. iii, 5
Acts xxvi,-5
Acts xxii, 8

evil,[2] which in time broke into activity and corrupted the whole mass. Man was made of flesh from the earth, with an earthly soul, and into him God breathed His own spirit, that he might be lord of all creation. But in the flesh of man there lurked also the impulse to evil, which needed to be kept in check by reason and obedience. Upon him one command was laid, under penalty of death, and this command he transgressed. The temptation came from Satan, who of old had rebelled against God and had drawn after him a host of spiritual beings. With the disobedience of Adam and Eve sin entered the world, spreading like an infectious disease, so that henceforth the flesh, with the material substance of which it was part, became synonymous with evil.[3] It is significant of this virtual identification of the flesh with sin, however the flesh may have been when first created, that Paul seems to have accepted a rabbinical myth of

[2] The *yetser hara'* of the rabbinical schools, with which they connect the *avath hanephesh*, desire of the soul, of the Old Testament. In the Greek of Paul this becomes *epithymia*, "desire," "covetousness" (*cf.* Rom. vii, 7 et seqq., and Ex. xx, 17).

[3] According to Bousset, *Die Religion des Judentums*, 464, the *yetser hara'*, impulse of evil, was never connected necessarily with the body, and Paul's conception of the flesh was rather Hellenistic than Judaic. I question the absoluteness of this statement, though certainly the location of evil in the flesh was not original with the Hebrews. At any rate Bousset admits that death and misfortune, as the consequences of evil, were inherited from Adam.

Eve's seduction by an embodied malign spirit, and of the mechanical transmission of evil down the generations of mankind by contact of body with body. And as man is born to sin, so he inherits the wages of sin, which is death. Somewhere beneath the earth lies the dark abyss of Sheol, to which every grave is, as it were, a gate; and thither the souls of men descend when divided from their fleshly organ and when the spirit of God in them returns to its source. It is not life in that weary abode, nor is it absolute annihilation, but a kind of life in death.

Thus the handiwork of God was given over to the dominion of the principalities and powers, the elements of the world, leagued together under Satan, the god of this age. Not man alone, Rom. viii, 22 but the whole creation groaneth and travaileth in pain together until now, under the bondage of corruption.

Meanwhile God would not suffer passively this perversion of His handiwork. To His chosen people of Israel He gave the Law, by obedience to which they might purge themselves of wickedness and redeem themselves from the reign of Satan. Even the gentile world was not left without intimations of His will and of the way of salvation: "For the invisible things of Him Rom. i, 20

from the creation of the world are clearly seen,
being understood by the things that are made,
even His eternal power and Godhead; so that
they are without excuse." But the nations have
followed rather the conceit of a wisdom that is
folly, falling into idolatry, changing the truth
of God into a lie, and worshipping the creature
more than the Creator. Even the Israelites, who
were abandoned to no uncertain light, preferred
for the most part the devices of their own hearts,
and the righteous are but a small people out of
all those who must face the wrath of God.

Jehovah is long-suffering and merciful, but
at the last His indignation will break forth
from the heavens like a devouring fire. In good
time, in the day of the Lord, He will send forth
His Messiah to put an end to the present age of
corruption, and to establish the new age of
glory. Now the Messiah whom Paul took over
from the eschatological belief of the age was a
spirit who had existed from the beginning, the
Son of God, through whom all things have their
being, the medium by which God communicated
with man in the old days as in the new. So close
was he to Deity that having the form of God he
thought it not robbery to be equal with God; yet
withal, however divine, he was not in the simple

I Cor. x, 4

Phil. ii, 6

absolute sense of the word God, for Paul makes I Cor. viii, 6 a clear distinction between the one supreme Deity and the eternal Son whose powers are delegated to him.[4] On that great day, without warning, without those indications of world-wide catastrophe which seem almost to have dropped from Paul's mind, Christ would appear suddenly in the sky, a spiritual being all of glory, radiant with light and a burning fire, surrounded by the angelic hosts and by the spirits of those just Israelites of old—Enoch and Abraham and Moses and Elijah—who had not gone down into Sheol but had been translated to the bosom of Jehovah. Then the last trumpet should be blown, and at the sound thereof the living righteous should be caught up, and out of the ghostly taverns of Hell the dead who had kept the Law should arise and join the triumphant throng. It is not easy for us, to whom the otherworld, if it exists at all, has receded into the limbo of meta-physical speculation, to comprehend the vivid realism of these beliefs of Paul and the early Christians; and only by a violent effort of the

[4] It is uncertain whether the phrase "God blessed for ever" (Rom. ix, 5) refers to Christ or to the Father. The simpler construction here would be to refer it to Christ, but the phrase is so common in Hebrew as a kind of parenthetical exclamation that the same use may have been carried over by Paul into his Greek. The reference of the words to Christ gives a meaning so out of harmony with Paul's views elsewhere, that critics commonly refer them to the Father.

imagination can we appreciate the longing yet trembling expectation with which, day after day and year after year, they must have raised their eyes to the empty sky and the curtain of the clouds for a sign of the Parusia, the Presence, as they called it. Some intimation of that feeling we get when we read Paul's words to the Thessalonians who, having trusted to the prophetic assurance that the living generation should not pass away before the end, were troubled to know what part their faithful dead should have in the triumph now so long delayed. Change "the dead in Christ" to "the righteous dead" and the language of Paul's reply might have been taken bodily out of one of the current apocalyptic books:

1 Thes. iv, 15 "For this we say unto you by the word of the Lord, that we which are alive and remain unto the coming of the Lord shall not prevent them which are asleep.

"For the Lord himself shall descend from heaven with a shout, with the voice of the archangel, and with the trump of God; and the dead in Christ shall rise first:

"Then we which are alive and remain shall be caught up together with them in the clouds, to meet the Lord in the air; and so shall we ever be with the Lord.

"Wherefore comfort ye one another with these words."

There, then, before a host of witnesses, the righteous from among the living and the dead shall appear before the judgement seat, to be rewarded in accordance with the deeds done in the body. God himself is the judge, the arbiter of things at the end as He is the source of all things in the beginning; and on that great day of assize the function of the Messiah is rather that of examiner and revealer, though Paul is not always consistent in his apportionment of the divine offices. The glory shining from the face of the Lord Christ will be as a light in the darkness, making manifest the secrets of all life; and it will be also as a scorching fire to separate the gold from the baser metal. "Every man's work shall be made manifest: for the day shall declare it, because it shall be revealed by fire; and the fire shall try every man's work of what sort it is. If any man's work abide which he hath built thereupon, he shall receive a reward. If any man's work shall be burned, he shall suffer loss: but he himself shall be saved; yet so as by fire." After the scorching and separation will come the crown of honour. The two words that run all through Paul's portrayal of the future are spirit

II Cor. v, 10

I Cor. iii, 13

and glory, which are but various expressions of the eternal life with God. In the presence of Christ's holiness all that is of the earth, the flesh of this body and the soul which animates it, shall shrivel away as in a great heat and vanish as darkness disappears before the light. What remains shall be raised in glory, but not the same; for as sun and moon and stars differ in glory, so will it be with the spirits of the just. Yet is the glory not of us though we wear it, nor the spirit of us though we live it; "but we all, with open face beholding as in a glass the glory of the Lord, are changed into the same image from glory to glory, even as by the Spirit of the Lord." It must be remembered always that to the imagination of Paul and the men for whom he wrote, these things were at once symbolical and very real; spirit, however refined of all the gross properties of the earth, was still in no sense of the word a metaphysical abstraction, but a kind of immaterial body moving in time and space, actually visible to the inner eye, visible indeed in happier moments to these eyes of the flesh. And the glory of the spirit is a light almost indistinguishable from the physical radiances of heaven.

Meanwhile for the wicked dead there is no

I Cor. xv, 40

II Cor. iii, 18

resurrection, and for the unrighteous living no
elevation to the throne of the celestial judge;
with the withdrawal of the children of light,
they, the children of darkness, the perishing
(*apollymenoi*), are abandoned to Satan the de-
stroyer. As their ways have been evil, their end is
death; as they have not within them the spirit of
God, which is life, their earthly tabernacle and
the soul that is of the flesh undergo the swift
decay of corruption. It is not clear whether the
state of the damned was conceived by Paul as
absolute annihilation or as a dull Lethean condition of inanity. Perhaps he did not discriminate between the two, as indeed to his ardent desire for the fullness of eternal life they would be
virtually synonymous; but from such passages
as II Thes. i, 9, it would appear that the death
of the soul was as final and complete as the
death of the body. At least it is notable that
he nowhere mentions hell as a place of lasting
torment.

The profoundest change in the eschatology
of the Jews had occurred in the period when,
perhaps under the spreading influence of Persian mythology, the serious enemies of Jehovah
and His Messiah were no longer regarded as the
rebellious nations of the earth, but as the dae-

monic powers of the air. This view had extended to the people, and certainly, as we have seen, was held by Jesus. To Paul it was intensely real, and in a sense the true drama of the Parusia was to take place after the winnowing of Sheol, when Christ and his celestial army were left to battle with the insurgent hosts of Satan. And in that work the saints also should take part, being accounted worthy to judge the world and its angels. This is the age of the Messianic reign, which shall endure, we are told, until Christ has put all his enemies under his feet. The last of these foes to be destroyed will be Death, who is no other than Satan himself, the personification at once of "spiritual wickedness in high places" and of the fatal working of corruption. In the majestic words of the apostle, borrowed and wrought together from Hosea and Isaiah, it is as though we heard the voices of the redeemed crying to one another across the spaces made empty of evil: "Death is swallowed up in victory. O death, where is thy sting? O grave, where is thy victory?" Then shall the kingdom of Christ also come to an end. Having subdued all things by the might of Jehovah, the Son himself shall surrender his reign to the Father, that God may be all in all.

The later apocalyptic writers wavered in their conception of the ultimate kingdom of Jehovah, describing it sometimes as a renewal of Paradise and a new Jerusalem upon this earth, and sometimes as a removal to the celestial spheres, or as a blend of the two. With Jesus the kingdom seems to have been placed pretty definitely on this earth, though the later Synoptics here and there may reflect another tradition. Paul again is vague. He speaks at one time as if the world, delivered from the sway of sin were to be recreated: "Old things are passed away; behold II Cor. v, 17 all things are new." At other times, particularly in the fifteenth chapter of First Corinthians, it appears rather as if the elements of the visible world were too far sunk in corruption to be saved, and should be wiped away altogether with their daemonic lords, leaving only a spiritual world of eternal life bathed in the glory of God's immediate presence.

So far the Christology of Paul contains nothing that we regard as specifically Christian; it can be matched image by image, almost word by word, from the various eschatological books current at the time, which the young Pharisee must have conned in his student days under Gamaliel. The burning question for the critic of Paul's life is to comprehend how this Messiah of the Jewish hope became identified with the historic Jesus; for the idea of a Messiah humiliated on the cross was a scandal utterly intolerable to the Pharisaic mind. The other apostles, as we know from Peter's protest after the confession at Caesarea Philippi, had felt this difficulty, and had been persuaded only by the vision of their risen Lord. How did Paul come to accept this belief in a Messiah, which, as he avows, was abhorrent to his whole being and had made him a fierce persecutor of the new sect? What is the secret of his conversion?

No doubt there were various external influences at work upon him, such as the beauty of the new Christian life and the exaltation of the martyred Stephen; all of which would have to be considered if we were writing a life of Paul. For our purpose we may reduce the matter to what, in technical language, might be called the inadequacy of the Jewish Christology to provide a reasonable soteriology. How, in a word, and by what right were men saved in this Messianic scheme which had been imposed upon the Mosaic Law? The soul that sinneth, it shall die, and, The wages of sin is death; and Paul could not overlook the fact that all men, not least the

Jews who possessed the Law, had fallen short of perfect obedience. Where, then, were the righteous who should stand in the day of judgement? Now the principle of vicarious punishment was familiar enough to the Hebrew mind; it entered into the idea of sacrifice, in particular into the annual ceremony of the scape-goat, and it had animated the marvellous and mystical imagery of the Prophet Isaiah. It had, however, never before been connected with the function of the Messiah; but what if these fanatics of the crucified Jesus were right, and, in the design of the Almighty, the Christ who was to overthrow the powers of evil must first bring salvation to men by vicariously suffering the penalty of death and so satisfying the Law?

With such thoughts as these we may suppose that Paul set out on that fateful journey to Damascus, troubled in his conscience, yet still "breathing out threatenings and slaughter against the disciples of the Lord." And on the way came the great light, and the vision of the glorified Jesus, and the voice: "Saul, Saul, why persecutest thou me?" For a season we are told that he went away into Arabia, partly, it may be, because for very shame he could not face immediately the men whom he had been reviling, Acts ix, 1 partly, and more specially, because he desired a period of solitude to adjust the new faith to his old belief. When he returned to Damascus, he brought with him a scheme of salvation, clearly outlined if not fully formed, and upon this was grafted a jealous conviction that God had chosen him to be the apostle to the gentiles.

The old Christology is retained, but with additions that develop it into a soteriology. Christ was still the Son of God existent for all eternity in the bosom of the Father; but as a spiritual being he could not take the place of those who were under the curse of God's wrath. Hence the need that he should be born as a mortal man in this sin-corrupted body of flesh, and so should undergo the full penalty of the Law, even the scandalous death of the cross. At the same time, though subject to all the weakness of flesh, he was saved by his spiritual nature from actual transgression; by reason of his perfect obedience he was raised by God from the dead and became "the first fruits of them that slept." The price of our redemption has been paid, and henceforth we belong to God. That is the new Gospel, the astounding truth that gave saving power to the old Messianism. It was this thought that led Paul to lay the whole stress of his teaching on the one fact of the cross and the Resurrection, and made him the preacher of Christ crucified and nothing else. The root of his religion, as we have seen, was a deep-seated aversion to transience and death and to that sinfulness which combines with death to form the horror of corruption. Only by remembering this can we understand those really frightful words with which he repudiated the imperfect Christians who saw the moral regeneration obtained by imitating Christ's example but denied the gift of eternal life:

"But if there be no resurrection of the dead, then is Christ not risen: 1 Cor. xv, 13,

"And if Christ be not risen, then is our preaching vain, and your faith is also vain.

"If in this life only we have hope in Christ, we are of all men most miserable."

Not without right has this passage been taken as the heart and centre of Paulinism.[5]

The mere notion of a crucified Messiah effects indeed a profound change in the eschatology which Paul learned in the schools, but it is still a change within and does not break through the scheme; and up to this point his conversion was only a more violent experience of what the other apostles had gone through before him. His origi-

[5] R. Kabisch, *Die Eschatologie des Paulus*.

nality begins with the attempt to explain the operation of the new soteriology, to give, that is, a rational account of the process by which man is vicariously saved through the death and resurrection of Christ. This is the field of his theology as distinguished from what may be called his Christology; and it is here that his rabbinical training left a mark on the Church which, as it seems to me, cannot be too deeply deplored. The subject is made difficult for exegesis by the fact that the apostle himself wavered among different theories which he never thoroughly harmonized, and which perhaps cannot be harmonized. More particularly the difficulty lies in the antithesis between the operation of grace and the operation of faith, which are, it might be said, the two poles of Paul's theology.

The simplest aspect of the doctrine of grace, and that which in Anselm's hands became classical for the Occident, may be designated the forensic; it hangs on the meaning of the word *dikaioô,* which is primarily, though not always or necessarily, a legal term signifying not "to justify," *i.e.,* "to make just," but "to pronounce just," "to acquit," as in a court of law. In this way Paul can say that we are "justified freely by his grace through the redemption that is in

Rom. iii, 24

Christ Jesus." It is a judicial process wherein the part of man remains purely passive. Men have sinned and are under condemnation; Christ by his death pays the penalty, and, the demands of justice being satisfied, God by a voluntary act of pardon proclaims the actual sinners to be free of guilt. This is a simple and comprehensible theory; but, taken at least in its baldest form as developed by an Anselm, it turns justice into arbitrary judgement, leaves the judge in rather a sorry plight, and reduces the whole scheme of salvation to a mockery. Why, if a man is merely pronounced just without any compensating act on his part, should Christ have died at all? Why should not God have pardoned man under the old dispensation of the Law without exacting the penalty from one who was innocent? And how, by such a process, is man delivered from the inner dominion of sin which to Paul was just as terrible as the outer penalty of death?

Such questions cannot easily be answered from the purely forensic point of view, and so, though this theory remains cardinal in Paul's theology, we find it modified, or supplemented, by a more metaphysical conception of the working of grace, which Paul developed from the eschatology of the age. Christ, the Son of God, concealed in the bosom of the Father, as it were, from eternity, was also the Son of man, and as such the prototype and consummation of humanity. The rabbinical scholars had taken the double account of man's creation in Genesis as the account of a double creation, and Philo had laid hold of this assumption of a double creation to impose on the Scripture a Platonic distinction between a phenomenal and an Ideal humanity. "There is a very great difference," he says, "between the man now formed [of the dust of the ground, Gen. ii, 7] and the man created before [Gen. i, 26] in the image of God. He who was now formed was sensible with specific qualities, consisting of body and soul, man and woman, mortal in nature; whereas the man created in the image of God was generic, a kind of Idea or seal, intelligible, incorporeal, neither male nor female, in nature incorruptible."[6] Something like this had passed into the Pauline theology, though without the Platonic colouring of the Alexandrian philosopher. It is now II Cor. iv, 4 Christ who in the full sense is the image of I Cor xv, 47 God, and as such may be called the second man, the Lord from Heaven, whereas the first man, Adam, was of the earth, earthy. As the Son of

[6] *De Opificio Mundi*, 134.

man, Christ is also the perfection of manhood
to which we can rise by participation in his
nature.

As the instrument of this participation grace
operates either through the mystical power of
solidarity or by the mechanical process of transference. Mystically, the race is regarded as a
unit, or as summed up in two representative
figures: "As in Adam all die, even so in Christ
shall all be made alive," and as the transgression
of one man brought death upon all, so by the
obedience of one all are justified. Mechanically,
by God's free gift the merit and spirit of Christ
are regarded as belonging to man, not by the
solidarity of Christ the man *with* men, but by a
transference from Christ *to* man. In this second
view the emphasis lies on the distinction between
the natural solidarity of mankind as created and
the attributed solidarity with Christ by grace;
and by an extension of this idea salvation becomes not so much an act of pardon as a process
of regeneration. "The first man Adam was made
a living soul, the last Adam was made a quickening spirit": we are the natural sons of Adam,
but now by the grace of God this quickening
spirit of the Son is transplanted into our soul
and cries, Abba, Father; we become thus the

Gal. iv, 19

I Cor. xv, 22
Rom. v, 17

I Cor. xv, 45

Gal. iv, 5

Rom. viii, 16 adopted sons of God, and if children, then heirs of eternal life and joint heirs with Christ; for which we have within us the spirit bearing witness.

It is by virtue of this mystico-mechanical aspect of Paul's theology, as we may term it, that he develops the sacramental side of religion, already pretty far advanced in the Church at the

Gal. iii, 27 time of his conversion. By the rite of baptism we "put on Christ." The immersion in the water and the emergence are not merely typical of our participation in the death and resurrection of Christ but do in some mysterious manner effect

Rom. vi, 3 that participation; we are baptized "into Christ," "buried with him" and with him "raised up from the dead"; we are "crucified with him," and "if we be dead with Christ we believe that we shall also

Gal. ii, 20 live with him." We no longer live to ourselves, but to Christ; rather, Christ lives in us. By the same extension the eucharist becomes, as it were, a renewal and perpetuation of the mystical union accomplished in baptism. This is figured in the

I Cor. x, 2 Old Testament by the baptism of the Israelites in the Red Sea and by the eating afterwards of the manna in the wilderness and the drinking of the spiritual Rock that followed them, which

was Christ.[7] And so, in set terms, Paul compares
the cup of blessing, which is communion of the
blood of Christ, and the broken bread, which
is communion of the body of Christ, with the
heathen table of devils, whereby, in the mystery
religions of the day, men believed they were
made one with their gods and purified for everlasting life.

The only logical, or one might rather say
decent, outcome of Paul's doctrine of justification by grace would be universalism. If the parallel between the first and the last man is carried
out consistently, then as all men have sinned in
Adam so all men should be saved in Christ. If
Christ by his death has satisfied the Law and by
the free gift of God his spirit is transferred into
us, so that we die and live with him; and, in general, whatever the *modus operandi,* if justification means merely that we are declared just or
made just by the voluntary fiat of God, then
surely there should be no discrimination of lost
and saved. Is God a respecter of persons? But
whatever the logic or decency of the argument,

[7] Philo Judaeus, *Leg. Alleg.* II, 86, has a similar allegory, though
of course not referred to the eucharist. The figure of the following Rock for the Messiah is probably drawn from some rabbinical source.

no Jew, and Paul least of all, would admit the conclusion of universalism; salvation belongs Rom. ix, 27 only to the remnant. And so we see Paul intro- Rom. viii, 30 ducing the doctrine of election: "Whom He did predestinate, them he also called; and whom he called, them he also justified; and whom he justified, them he also glorified." Not a pleasant view, this of an omnipotent Deity arbitrarily creating for glory or damnation, and restricting his compassionate love to the small band of the elect; and Paul himself, taking a metaphor familiar to the prophets, anticipates such an ob- Rom. ix, 20 jection. "Nay but, O man, who art thou," he says, "that repliest against God? Hath not the potter power over the clay, of the same lump to make one vessel unto honour, and another unto dishonour?" To which the vessel might reply: "O Paul, he may have the power, but if this clay be the sentient souls of men, hath he the right?" No, this metaphor of the potter is one of the most heart-sickening shifts of a false theology. I would not presume to question the design of Providence, for God's ways are not as our ways; but to ask me to believe that a just and omnipotent Deity chooses to fashion human beings to the end of dishonour is to quench the only light I have in this dark world and to make a mockery of my moral sense. I should prefer to leave those ultimate causes untouched in their remote obscurity; but if you force me to decide, I would rather waive the omnipotence than the goodness of God.

And Paul himself, I think, felt that this theory of free grace, which came to him ready made from the rabbinical schools of theology, dishonoured God and contradicted that innate sense of human responsibility which is deeper than logic. And so all through his epistles, side by side with the doctrine of justification by grace and interwoven with it, runs the other doctrine of justification by faith.

Now the principle of faith was not discovered by Paul, any more than the principle of grace. As he himself points out, it was really by faith that Abraham had been saved under the old dispensation. In the apocalyptic books it plays an increasingly important part.[8] It underlies the teaching of Jesus, and is the significance of his call to repentance. But however the predecessors of Paul may have seen the need of faith in religion, it is no more than fair to say that to

[8] Brückner, *Die Entstehung der paulinischen Christologie*, 217, gives abundant references to the doctrine of faith in the apocalyptic literature. The matter is excellently summed up in H. St. J. Thackeray's little manual *The Relation of St. Paul to Contemporary Jewish Thought*, 90 et seqq.

Paul belongs the credit of making Christianity essentially the religion of faith. And this revolution, if the word be not too strong, was effected by the intensity and intimacy of his personal conviction; his faith, so considered, was the positive outcome of that instinctive revolt from transience and death which gave strength to his longing for permanence and life.

Perhaps the subtlest point of Paul's whole system is his use of the principle of faith to adjust the original Jewish conception of the Law to the newer, and in large measure imported, mythology of the Last Things. Adam and Eve, he argues, were under a special command, by the transgression of which they brought sin and death into the world. But from the time of Adam to the time of Moses there was no Law. Sin, indeed, passed by the inheritance of the flesh from generation to generation, but men sinned unwittingly. They suffered the penalty of death, but had no pangs of conscience. Then the Law was given, and with the Law came knowledge. Henceforth men suffered both physically and morally, physically by the subjection of the body to death, morally by the sting of remorse. In a way their state was worse than it had been before the revelation on Sinai, since the Law, while doubling the consequences of evil, provided no means of escape. It might promise salvation through perfect obedience, but it was external and could not effect a change in the corrupt inheritance which rendered such obedience impossible: "As it is written, there is none righteous, no not one." If Law were all, then Paul would say that it was better for men in the old state, when at least they might comfort themselves with the Epicurean indifference: "Let us eat and drink, for tomorrow we die." But the Law by awakening conscience prepared the way for the operation of faith. It was only by reason of the misery of remorse that men turned from themselves, in whom there was no help, to God and His offer of salvation in the vicarious death of Christ. Faith is just that inner law of our being, as distinguished from the external act of grace, whereby of our own will we appropriate to ourselves the victory of Christ over sin and death. By faith we become no longer ourselves, but are made one with the spirit of Christ in us, so that on the day of judgement we have that which shall stand before the wrath of God.

There is in Paul's concentration of faith upon the crucifixion and resurrection an unfortunate

Rom. iii, 10
Ps. xlv, 3

I Cor. xv, 32

element which has left a trail of morbid sentiment all through the centuries of Christianity.
A wholesome mind, for instance, must feel
something like disgust at the letters of a Cather-
ine of Siena, with their sickly brooding on the
"blood" and the "cross." But in principle the
doctrine of faith springs from a sound psychology. It is by belief in another that we are transformed into likeness with him, and it is by virtue of the law of imitation through faith that the
morality of Paul, when freed from disturbing
influences, becomes almost identical with that of
the Gospels. But for the omission of one word,
Paul's list of the fruits of the Spirit might
be taken as a summary of the Sermon on the
Gal. v, 22   Mount: "Love, joy, peace, longsuffering, gen-
tleness, goodness, faith, meekness, temperance."
One word only we miss, "purity," but elsewhere
Paul lays full stress on the value of things that
Phil. iv, 8   are pure. And, more generally, it is to Paul we
owe perhaps the finest compendium of gospel
Gal. v, 6   morality ever written: "Faith which worketh
through love," or, as it may be translated literally, "faith working within through love."

The matter is not quite so simple when we
come to the element of otherworldliness in Paul's
faith. It has been seen that his setting of the re-

ligious life depends on a kind of spiritual realism. The spirit of Christ, which we appropriate
by faith, was to him a substantial body, subtler
than the body of the flesh and for the present
invisible, yet in a way true substance. So the act
of resurrection was interpreted bluntly as the
release of this new man from the old Adam of
flesh and soul, and its manifestation in a glory
scarcely distinguishable from the physical splen-
dours of the sky. In like manner faith meant the
belief in a series of events which are merely the
prolongation of the facts of history. The appearance of Christ, the tribunal of judgement,
the abolition of the powers of evil, the surrender
of the kingdom to God, are all conceived realis-
tically; they differ from the captivity and de-
liverance of Israel only as the future differs
from the past. At times, indeed, this simplicity
of faith may be broken by something that sounds
like the note of true Hellenism. "Eye hath not   I Cor. ii, 9
seen," Paul writes, "nor ear heard, neither have
entered into the heart of man the things which
God hath prepared for them that love him. But
God hath revealed them unto us by his Spirit."
Paul's account of the Last Things should not
be taken with too gross a literalness (against
this he himself utters a warning) ; nevertheless

his realization of the otherworld is only an imperfect vision of what one day shall be seen extended in space and transacted in time as surely I Cor. xiii, 12 as the events of this phenomenal life: "For now we see through a glass darkly, but then face to face."

Now it is a curious fact that the German writers who make the most of Paul's theology are also most resolute in discarding his spiritual realism, for which they would substitute a spiritual metaphysic. And with this change there runs all through German exegesis, even when most completely sceptical, the assumption, if not the open boast, that the genuine spirituality of religion begins with Luther and is a unique creation of the Teutonic brain. Any one familiar with the literature of the subject will vouch for this statement, and I need quote only a single passage:

"Just here lies the deepest peculiarity of the Pauline and Jewish mode óf thought as compared with our [German] present mode. We separate sharply our scientific world-knowledge and the hypotheses based thereon from our religious thought and feeling, and by doing this we remove the sphere of religious life out of the region of objective fact into the region of inner experience, out of the categories of reality into the categories of manner and value. For Paul on the contrary religion is a relation between God and man based on facts and realized through facts. Religion and world-knowledge are combined."[9]

The difference, it will be seen, lies in the use of the imagination. In the realism of St. Paul the imagination works unconsciously or involuntarily; the figures which clothe for him the life of glory are regarded as substantial realities. In the metaphysical theology of the German stamp the things of the spirit are kept apart from the imagination, or, if the fancy enters at all into play, it is a kind of voluntary and conscious poetry. This means practically that to the modern mind things of the spirit must remain unexpressed and, as a consequence, unreal, for the good reason that, as we are mentally constituted, we possess no other mode of expressing and realizing such things than just the spatial and temporal figures of the imagination. There is, one must admit, a profound embarrassment here: on the one hand the realism of St. Paul, which imparts significance and vigour to religious hope, but which can scarcely be maintained intact against the dissolving force of reflection;

[9] Brückner, *Op. cit.*, 11.

on the other hand the metaphysics derived from
Luther through Kant, which leaves the religious
life *in vacuo,* so to speak, a mere category of
thought with no basis in fact. We cannot believe
literally in the Last Things as St. Paul believed
in them; belief under the condition of German
metaphysics means virtually belief in nothing.
The eschatological faith of St. Paul, if honestly professed today, would be superstition;
faith of the Luthero-Kantian sort, despite the
pretensions of German theology, is void of content and in practice passes into an agnostic materialism. I see no escape from this dilemma save
into a kind of symbolism which admits the complete duality of spirit and matter, Ideas and
phenomena, yet at the same time knows that the
figures of the imagination may correspond with
the facts of the inner life, and hence may be profoundly true. That was the essential character
of the Platonic philosophy, which succeeded in
making the laws of the otherworld at once consciously imaginative and ethically realistic; and,
as we have seen, this was the turn given to the
eschatology of the kingdom and the Parusia by
the master thinkers of the Church, building on
the foundation laid by Paul. Such a symbolic use
of the imagination, hovering midway between

realism and metaphysics, may seem to suffer
from the instability attendant upon all compromises; it does certainly require an effort of
the will to prevent the mind from slipping into
one of the two extremes of materialism or metaphysical vacuity. We shall learn, as we go on,
that the great advance of Christianity over Platonism lies in the addition of a new element of
religion,—faith in the dual nature of a person,
which demands no such compromise of the imagination as does faith in the dualism of things.

At any rate the weakness of Paul's position
does not arise from his spiritual realism; it lies
rather in the region of pure theology. The grace
of God is a living fact, and the faith of man is
a living fact; but by the vehemence of his logic
Paul set up a feud between two fierce abstrac-
tions, absolute grace and absolute faith, which
corresponds to nothing in mortal experience and
has been the prolific source of schism and disaster. By this door entered the old Stoic mischief
of determinism and liberty, and from the revival
of Paulinism under St. Augustine the theologians of the West have never ceased wrangling

> Of providence, foreknowledge, will, and fate,
> Fixt fate, free will, foreknowledge absolute, . . .
> Vain wisdom all and false philosophy.[10]

[10] *Paradise Lost,* ii, 559 et seqq.

When the clash comes in Paul's mind between the determinism of grace and the liberty of faith, it is grace that triumphs, and under this domination of what is really a form of monistic rationalism faith ceases to be the voluntary response of the human soul to the call of the divine and fades away into a mere state of passive receptivity; it is no longer the inner principle of otherworldliness working itself out in righteousness, but as the arbitrary gift of God, like grace, is accounted by God for righteousness.

Hence arises that deplorable antagonism between faith and works, faith and the Law, which has no ground in psychology and should never have intruded into religion. In his eschatological scheme Paul had contrived, with rather far-fetched ingenuity, it may be, to make a place for faith as the birth of a conscience troubled by the impossibility of fulfilling the Law. In his theology this sequence is broken, and the Law becomes, not a preparation for faith, but its opponent; not only is there no justification for man from the works of the Law, but if justification were possible by the Law, then had Christ died to no purpose. This antagonism, I repeat, has no basis in the facts of our inner experience and is unchristian. Jesus had made a distinction between the ritual and the morality of the Law, and while he had rejected the Pharisaic abuse of ritual, had developed and deepened but never by a word repudiated the principle of legal morality. Always a man is judged by his fruits, and there is no thought of separating faith and works, not to mention any antipathy between them. Paul by his conception of works virtually lumps ritual and morality together in one indiscriminate condemnation as opposed to the imputed righteousness of faith.

Temporarily the determinism of Paul's theology, like the similar creed among the Mohammedans, may have acted as a strong tonic to the will; but in the end, as we see in the results of the German Reformation and in the Presbyterian church of England, his influence has been to drive the mind away from the dualism of religion into a pure naturalism or into the halfway house of a humanitarian Christianity.

It is noteworthy that the speculation of the East simply passed over this aspect of the Pauline doctrine. In all the Greek Fathers you will find scarcely a trace of that grand debate over grace and faith and works and justification which so occupied the Western Church. Their interest was concentrated almost exclusively on the dogma of the Incarnation, with which the truth of Christianity as a world-religion stands or falls.

CHAPTER X

THE FOURTH GOSPEL

THE first sensation of a critical reader on passing from Paul to John is likely to be that of
entering a new world of religious emotion. In
place of the intense personal note and concentrated passion of the epistles one finds one's
self suddenly in an atmosphere of impersonal
and rather relaxed contemplation. And with
this change there goes a profound difference in
the presentation of the gospel. Paul continues
the Messianic eschatology of the Synoptics, en-
larging the supernatural elements of the drama
on the one side, while on the earthly side cen-
tring his interest almost exclusively on the crucifixion and resurrection. In John, on the contrary, the eschatology is virtually eliminated;
and in place of the expected Parusia the Messiah appears as the Logos, whose life on earth
is only one incident in the eternal self-revelation
of God. Faith, also, develops in a new direction,
taking now the colour of Greek philosophy and

Alexandrian *gnôsis*. Of the writer of the Epistles we know something; who wrote the fourth Gospel, and what was his relation to Christ and the early Church?

Now we must, I fear, give up the old orthodox view that the Gospel, at least as we have it, is the work of John the son of Zebedee. I know that a few learned scholars, chiefly of the English school, still cling to the traditional belief; but it simply will not do. To take a crucial instance: according to the record of Mark nowhere does Jesus make a public confession of his Messiahship; more than that, on two critical occasions, the Transfiguration and the Petrine confession, he earnestly implores his disciples to keep the matter secret. In the fourth Gospel, on the contrary, the apostles knew him from the first as the lamb of God and the Messiah, and there is no hint of reticence. If Mark is historical, then the narrative of the fourth Gospel misrepresents the truth, and in a matter so fundamental to the conception of Christ's life that we are obliged to discredit it as the work of an apostle. Every canon of sound criticism forces us to the conclusion that John is not the author of the book that bears his name. Yet, on the other hand, for no one of the other Gospels

Jn. 1, 36, 41

have we equally valid testimony to its reputed
authorship. Unquestionably the editor who ap-
pended the last chapter took the "disciple whom
Jesus loved" to be John the son of Zebedee, and
regarded him as the writer of the book. Even
stronger is the evidence from Polycarp through
Irenaeus, bishop of Lyons in the latter part of
the second century. In his youth Polycarp had
been a hearer of John, probably at Ephesus.
This information we get directly from Irenaeus,
and there ought to be no doubt that by John he
meant the apostle. "Polycarp," he says, "was
instructed by apostles and was intimate with
many of those who had seen our Lord. . . .
And him (Polycarp) we also saw in our early
youth, for he lived to a great age. . . . Always
he taught what he had learned from the apostles; which things also are the tradition of the
Church."[1] Now Irenaeus had a friend named
Florinus who in old age was bitten by heresy,
and this is how Irenaeus writes to him by way
of reproof:

"As a boy I saw you in Asia with Polycarp, dis-
tinguishing yourself in the royal court and en-
deavouring to gain his good will. Those things
I remember better than recent events; for what
we learn in youth is knit into our very soul and
[1] *Adv. Haer.*, II, iii, 4.

grows with it, so that I can tell the place where the blessed Polycarp sat when he discoursed, and his very comings-in and goings-out, and the character of his life, and the appearance of his body, and his public lectures, and how he spoke of his association with John and the others who had seen the Lord, and how he repeated their words and told us what he had heard from them. . . . And all things that Polycarp related were in harmony with the Scriptures."[2]

By Scriptures Irenaeus means the Gospels, in this case particularly the fourth Gospel, which elsewhere he attributes to John.[3] The point is that his attribution of the fourth Gospel to the apostle does not depend on loose tradition, but is authenticated by the correspondence of the book with the matter which came to him orally from a direct hearer of John. Such testimony cannot be lightly laid aside, but how can we reconcile it with the view of the Gospel forced upon us by criticism?

If there is any key to this problem it is to be found in the composite character of the material in the book. I am aware of the danger of such a recourse to explain difficulties, and know that

2 Eusebius, *Ec. Hist.*, v, 20.
3 *Adv. Haer.*, III, i, 2. "Afterwards John the disciple of the Lord, he who lay on his breast, also himself published the Gospel, while he was living at Ephesus."

indiscreet critics lay hold of such hypotheses to indulge in all sorts of wild conjectures; yet in the case of Matthew and Luke we can see with something like certainty how the authors worked together the narrative of Mark and the collection of Jesus' sayings which we call Q, or the Matthean Logia, and it should seem to be pretty clear that something of the same kind has occurred in the composition of our John. Here again we can discriminate several strata.

The writer of the fourth Gospel as it now stands would appear to have had the synoptic Gospels before him, and to have borrowed from them much of the framework of his narrative. As an illustration of his method we may take the story of the anointing of Jesus, which is demonstrably constructed from passages in all three of the Synoptics. This story Matthew had taken over from Mark with only a few verbal changes. In both Gospels the scene is laid at Bethany in the house of Simon the leper, and in both an unnamed woman pours the precious contents of an alabaster box on Jesus' head. In Luke the woman becomes a sinner, and is represented as washing the feet of Jesus with her tears and wiping them with the hairs of her head, while anointing them with the myrrh. But Luke also

Mt. xxvi, 6
Mk. xiv, 3

vii, 36

x. 38

knows of Martha and Mary, the friends of Jesus who dwelt in a certain village (Bethany is not named), and he describes Martha as "cumbered about much service," while Mary sat at Jesus' feet and listened to his words. This is the material at the disposal of our fourth evangelist, and we can see exactly how he uses his documents. Jn. xii, 1 ments. In this account the scene is laid at Bethany, but is transferred from the house of Simon to the home of the sisters, where, as in Luke, Martha is said to have "served." It is now Mary who brings the ointment, which is described in epithets combined from Matthew and Mark,[4] but which she pours upon his feet as in Luke. The rest of the story is a composite from Matthew and Mark, with no reference to the *quia multum amavit,* etc., of Luke. The evidence shows unmistakably that the author of the fourth Gospel in this case was not drawing on his own memory or on oral tradition, but composed his account with deliberate selection from the written documents as we have them. Most of his narrative displays the same method, though it is probable that he also had at his disposal other sources, written or oral, which have been lost.

[4] Matthew, αλάβαστρον μύρου βαρυτίμου (or πολυτίμου) ; Mark, ἀλάβαστρον μύρου νάρδου πιστικῆς (a rare and obscure word) πολυτελοῦς; John, λίτραν μύρου νάρδου πιστικῆς πολυτίμου.

Thus the Synoptics make no mention of any visit to Jerusalem until the end of Jesus' ministry, whereas in the fourth Gospel he goes up to the city three times. Quite possibly in this our evangelist follows a true tradition which for some reason unknown to us was overlooked by his predecessors. Again, in placing the Last Supper on the day before the Passover, he would appear to be correcting the synoptic date from independent knowledge.

One object apparently of the evangelist in adding a fourth to the already existing Gospels was to present the life of Jesus in such a light as to meet various heresies and conflicting sects. We know, for example, that some time after the death of Jesus there persisted at Ephesus a party who professed to be adherents of John the Baptist,[5] and the evangelist alters the synoptic account of the baptism and elsewhere goes out of his way to emphasize the fact that John was only a forerunner and openly acknowledged the Messiahship of Jesus. More important was the nascent sect of the Gnostics in the early years of the second century; and against their doctrine the evangelist upholds on the one hand the filial relation of Christ to the one and only supreme

[5] Acts xviii, 24 et seq.; xix, 3 et seq. See also Justin, *Dial.* lxxx, 2, and *Clementine Recognitions*, i, 54, 60.

God, while enforcing on the other hand his veritable humanity in the flesh. It is probably also in view of the docetic tendency of Gnosticism that he omits all mention of the virgin birth and the fatherhood of the Holy Ghost. At the same time, despite his antipathy to the more fantastic aspects of the growing heresy, there are signs that he himself had not entirely escaped its influence. For instance his constant discrimination between those who are of God, or the Spirit, and those who are of the world, between the children of light and the sons of darkness, is quite in line with the Gnostic classification.

Primarily, however, the purpose of the evangelist was to enforce the divine nature of Christ. That is manifest in every line and accent of the book; but the most significant feature of this open deification of Jesus is the writer's attitude towards miracles. These are no longer chiefly acts of healing as in the Synoptics, nor, except in one or two passages which have been inadvertently carried over from an earlier source, does Jesus show any reluctance to pose as a wonder-worker. On the contrary miracles are raised to the place of first importance as proofs of supernatural authority. Jesus begins his ministry, not as in Matthew and Mark with the gospel cry, "Repent, for the kingdom of heaven is at hand," but first "manifested forth his glory" by a feat of magic at Cana of Galilee,—

Nympha pudica Deum vidit, et erubuit, . . .[6]

and by that display won the belief of his disciples. So, on healing the man born blind, he does not say, as in Mark on a similar occasion to the man sick of a palsy, "Thy sins be forgiven thee"; his words now are: "Neither hath this man sinned, nor his parents, but that the works of God should be made manifest in him." These are not isolated instances of the fourth Gospel, but represent a conscious design to set the life of Christ in a framework of thaumaturgy, "for the glory of God, that the Son of God might be glorified thereby."

Mk. ii, 5

Jn. ix, 8

Jn. xi, 4

When, however, one turns to the many discourses of Jesus contained in the Gospel, one is struck by a certain discord with the spirit of the narrative parts. Here the dominant tone is no longer signs and works (*sêmeia, erga*), but words (*rêmata*), and the authority claimed by Jesus is no longer based on the miraculous nature of what he does but on the saving power of what he says. The keynote is given in the reply of Peter when Jesus asks the Twelve whether

[6] Crashaw, *Epigrammata Sacra.*

Jn. vi, 68 they too will go away: "Lord, to whom shall we
go? thou hast the words (*rêmata*) of eternal
life." Evidently in the mind of the Master, as
he shows himself in the discourses, the planting
of these words of everlasting life, the gospel of
salvation, the delivery of this message from the
Father, are his divinely appointed task, as they
iv, 84 are God's work: "My meat is to do the will of
him that sent me, and to finish his work," and
vi, 29 "This is the work of God, that ye believe on him
whom he hath sent."

Hence the strong impression that in the fourth
Gospel we have two discordant views of the authority asserted by Jesus, coming from different
sources; inevitably one is led to conjecture that
the evangelist, with his notions of a thaumaturgic being, has imbedded in his narrative a set
of speeches which came to him by a separate
tradition, and which present quite another sort
of Christ. To a certain extent he has altered the
speeches to his own taste, but not thoroughly,
and in some places we can put our finger on the
suture, where the patching is clumsy. In the
actual language of Jesus "works" and "words,"
as we have seen, were virtually synonymous,
whereas over and over again they are interpreted by the evangelist as if they were con-
x, 88 trasted. So he reports Christ as saying: "Though

ye believe not me (*i.e.,* my words), believe the works." Again in the discourse at the Last Supper we have the genuine tradition preserved in the sentence: "The words that I speak unto you I speak not of myself; but the Father that dwelleth in me, he doeth the works." Here, evidently, words and works are synonymous. But in the next chapter the evangelist sets them apart by what appears to be an addition of his own. "If I had not come and spoken unto them, they had not had sin," he found in his source, and repeats; and then, obsessed by the notion of signs, he adds: "If I had not done among them the works which none other man did, they had not had sin."

xiv, 10

xv, 22

xv, 24

These are some of the indications of the manner in which the fourth Gospel was put together. But the how is not so important as the whence. What is the origin of these speeches, or Logia as we may call them, incorporated into the evangelist's framework? Obviously, he himself, though he may have altered, did not compose them; did they then come to him by written or oral tradition, and who or what lies behind them? Above all, do they perchance go back to the Apostle John? That is a question to which, I am afraid, no positive answer can be given; but I think we can reach a fair probability. In the first place, if these Logia are read apart from their context and compared with the longer epistle attributed to John, the similarities of style are such as to strike the most casual critic; and indeed it is pretty generally conceded that the epistle and these sections of the Gospel come from the same hand, or at least from the same school. Certain details of language run through both. The ideas are alike, except for the difference explicable by the fact that in one case the author speaks in his own name, whereas in the other he professes to be the reporter of things remembered. And, more especially, the mental procedure is identical. In both the epistle and the Logia one is impressed by a childlike simplicity of mind, a naïveté degenerating at times into something very close to garrulity, which suggests the loving and beautiful old age of an untrained intellect. The writer wanders back and forth, he repeats himself and fumbles about his theme, he seems scarcely to understand what he is trying to say; and then—and this is equally characteristic of both documents—of a sudden there flashes out through the verbiage an isolated sentence, clear, ringing, condensed, profound, unforgettable. It is a word of the Master, we whisper, and a thrill goes to our very heart. Such particularly are the sayings scattered through the long and confused discourse at the Last Supper:

"Have I been so long time with you, and yet hast thou not known me, Philip?"

"Peace I leave with you, my peace I give unto you: not as the world giveth, give I unto you. Let not your heart be troubled, neither let it be afraid."

"A little while, and ye shall not see me: and again, a little while, and ye shall see me."

"In the world ye shall have tribulation; but be of good cheer; I have overcome the world."

"This is my commandment, That ye love one another, as I have loved you."

Now I hold it inconceivable that the author of the rambling speeches and of the epistle, not to mention the final redactor of the Gospel, should have minted these coins of pure gold; they derive from a deeper source and a finer brain. All the signs indicate that we have here the written record of one who for many years had cherished in memory some of the great utterances of Jesus, until they had grown into the texture of his soul, but who of himself had no faculty of concentrated thought or of consecutive composition. It does not follow necessarily that the author of the epistle and the speeches was the Apostle John; but such an attribution accords well with what we know otherwise of the apostle's latter years at Ephesus,[7] and it is the only theory that explains the traditional authorship of the Gospel supported by the evidence of Irenaeus. It is perfectly natural that the work as a whole should be associated with the name of John, if the speeches, which form the kernel of the book, were from his hand.

[7] The balance of the evidence for and against John's residence in Ephesus as an old man seems to me strongly for the affirmative.

Mark x, 35 et seqq. After the request of James and John to sit at the right and left hand of the Lord in the kingdom, Jesus replies: "Ye shall indeed drink of the cup that I drink of," etc. This is taken, as a *vaticinium ex eventu*, to prove that both brothers suffered martyrdom. But, even so, it does not follow necessarily that they suffered at the same time and place.

Acts xii, 1 et seqq., mentions the martyrdom of James and the imprisonment of Peter by Herod. This occurred at Jerusalem in the year 44. Strange that the martyrdom of John is not mentioned, if it happened then. Eduard Meyer (III, 177) who will not accept the Ephesian tradition, is driven to the desperate remedy of suggesting a corruption in the text of Acts.

A fragment of Papias, ca. A.D. 130, states that "John the theologue and James his brother were slain by the Jews." Again, it does not follow that they were slain at the same time and place; and the epithet "theologue" shows that John was the reputed author of works composed after the year 44. If Papias, something of a blunderhead, is correct on one point, why not on both?

Ignatius refers to Paul's presence in Ephesus, but not to John's. Polycarp in his letter makes no mention of John there. But the argument *ex silentio* is notoriously weak.

A Syrian manuscript of the fifth century gives December 27 as the day of the martyrdom of both John and James. But against this evidence can be set a Latin manuscript of the ninth century which states that according to Papias the Gospel was dictated *ab Iohanne adhuc in corpore constituto.*

Justin, who dwelt at Ephesus about 135, makes John the author of the Apocalypse, which must have been written after the year 44 (*Dial.* lxxxi, 4). Clement of Alexandria has a long story, bearing the manifest stamp of veracity, of John's activity at Ephesus as an old man. And, not to delay over later traditions, there is the testimony of Polycarp, through Irenaeus, which seems to me irrefragable.

At any rate, without attempting to draw the line too sharply, we can be assured that the fourth Gospel consists of three strands: (1) the narrative framework, (2) a body of rambling discourses attributed to Jesus, which came to the evangelist in the form of oral or, more probably, written tradition, and (3) imbedded in these discourses a number of sayings of Jesus himself. If this be true, we possess in the speeches attributed to Jesus a body of tradition comparable to the source Q of Matthew and Luke, only more diluted by extraneous comment and modified by longer retention in memory. And further, if John be the source of this tradition, then there would be three great apostolic authorities for our knowledge of Christ: the Gospel of Mark (probably inspired by Peter), the Logia of Matthew (if the Q of the first and third Gospels come from him), and the Logia of John. The evidence for this triple authority is sufficient to satisfy my own mind.[8]

Waiving the thaumaturgic framework of the

8 I have said nothing about the attribution of the fourth Gospel to another John of Ephesus, called the presbyter as distinguished from the apostle. I am inclined to regard this whole matter of the presbyter as a mare's nest. But, granted that John the presbyter, not the apostle, was the author of the Logia, the thesis I am supporting would remain intact. C. F. Burney has recently argued that the book was originally written in Aramaic, probably at Antioch and at a comparatively early date. But, again, this theory, if accepted, is not irreconcilable with the double authorship.

unknown evangelist, we have yet the real problem of the Gospel in the Logia which pretend to report the words of Jesus. How does the author of these Logia present the speaker? The complexity of the question will be shown if we group together a few texts bearing on various aspects of this presentation.

As messenger:—

"He whom God hath sent speaketh the words of God."

"Ye both know me, and ye know whence I am: and I am not of myself, but he that sent me is true, whom ye know not. But I know him: for I am from him."

"I speak that which I have seen with my Father."

"He that sent me is with me."

"As thou, Father, art in me, and I in thee, that they also may be one in us."

"He that hath seen me hath seen the Father."

"I and my Father are one."

As life:—

"The living Father hath sent me, and I live by the Father."

"The words that I speak unto you, they are spirit, and they are life."

"He that believeth on me hath eternal life."

"This is life eternal, that they might know

thee the only true God, and Jesus Christ, whom thou hast sent."

"I am the way, the truth, and the life."

As food and drink:—

"Whosoever drinketh of this water shall thirst again: but whosoever drinketh of the water that I shall give him shall never thirst."

"If any man thirst, let him come unto me, and drink."

"I am the bread of life: he that cometh to me shall never hunger; and he that believeth on me shall never thirst."

"Whoso eateth my flesh, and drinketh my blood, hath eternal life."

As light:—

"I must work the works of him that sent me, while it is day."

"And this is the condemnation, that light is come into the world, and men loved darkness rather than light."

"I am the light of the world."

Now in all these groups—which might be multiplied—it will be seen that the procedure is the same: they each set the person of Jesus in, so to speak, an ascending scale. He is the messenger of God, he has special knowledge of God, he himself is the substance of that message as bearing the revelation of God, he is the Son of God, he is God,—which of these grades represents the exact claim of the speaker as it abode in the memory of the reporter? They may, of course, be interpreted in such a manner as to merge them together and leave no necessity of choice. Thus, at one end of the scale, the title of messenger ("one sent") might be taken as merely a lower way of stating the condescension of Deity, or, at the other end of the scale, the oneness of Father and Son might be regarded as no more than a hyperbolical expression of the complete submission of a human will to God's; but I think that an unprejudiced reading of the Gospel will not so easily slur over the different degrees of pretension. In part the disparity may be explained by supposing that some of the phrases have been added by the evangelist who worked the Logia into the Gospel as it stands, and in so doing edited them, more or less, to suit his purpose. But in the main I suspect that the confusion goes back to the original author of the speeches, who had a habit of running text and comment together in such a manner that we can no longer detect where memory ends and interpretation begins. In the course of many years it may have become difficult even for him to distinguish between what Christ actually said and

what, under the spell of the Resurrection, had
germinated in the hearer's mind.

Indications of this double work of amalgama-
tion at the hands of the author and editor would
seem to be left uncovered in the account of the
raising of Lazarus, which is peculiar to, and
highly characteristic of, the fourth Gospel. As   xi, 1
that story now reads, Jesus is said to have heard
of the illness of Lazarus, whom he loved, from
the sisters Martha and Mary, who summoned
him to their help; but instead of going immediately, he lingered for several days. His delay
might have been explained on the ground that
Bethany was in the vicinity of Jerusalem, and
exposed to the enmity of those who were seeking his life. But according to the text his going
was deferred rather for the greater manifestation of the glory of the Son of God, to the intent
that his disciples might believe. Now all this,
the miracle deliberately planned in support of
Christ's divine claims, is quite in keeping with
the idea of the evangelist, whereas it is not at all
in the spirit of the author of the Logia; nor has
any commentator ever succeeded in explaining
the bitter grief of Jesus over one for whose death
he had deliberately waited and who was to come

forth from the tomb at a word. Pretty clearly
what has happened is this. In the Logia the death
of Lazarus was given as the occasion of a discourse of Jesus on the assurance of eternal life,
spoken to comfort the sorrowing sisters. Nor on
such a supposition would there be anything inconsistent in the tears of the comforter; they
would be the natural expression of that pain
which pierces the heart at the sight of death,
with its terrible silence and its rending of human
ties, no matter how strong the hope of another
life may be. This event the evangelist has transformed into a miracle after his taste, while awkwardly leaving traces of the true situation. And
the words of Christ have undergone a double
change at his hands and at those of the original
reporter. Martha, we are told, greeted Jesus
with the loving complaint, "Lord, if thou hadst
been here, my brother had not died"; and Jesus
answered, "Thy brother shall rise again." So
far the words have the ring of authenticity; they
are quite in the vein of Mark, and point not to a
coming miracle, but to the hope of the kingdom
which the Synoptics make the centre of Jesus'
preaching. The continuation also may be the
language of Jesus: "He that believeth in me
(*i.e.,* in my words), though he were dead, yet

shall he live; and whosoever liveth and believeth in me shall never die." That is the tone of the Logia, the medial grade, as we have seen, in all the groups; but of the accompanying sentence we cannot be so confident: "I am the resurrection." That belongs with the extreme of the groups, and like the kindred saying, "I am the way, the truth, and the life," would appear to convey rather the reflection of John than the actual remembered words of Jesus. And then comes what almost certainly can be attributed to the editor who has altered the story into a scene of wonder-working: "Said I not unto thee, if thou wouldest believe, thou shouldest see the glory of God?" Surely that is not the true sequence to the simple words of comfort, "Thy brother shall rise again." And surely, if Mark's account of the Messianic secret is historical, no eye-witness could have represented Martha as exclaiming: "Thou art the Christ."

The story of Lazarus offers a kind of epitome of the whole Gospel, showing the different strands in its composition and the double purpose that runs through it. But there yet remains an important factor to be considered: what shall we say of the Prologue, with its solemn strain of philosophy: "In the beginning was the Word"?

Now in the first place it can be said that in thought these verses fall in with verses from the body of the Gospel to form an ascending scale like the groups already quoted. Thus:—

"Thy word (*logos*) is truth."

"If a man keep my sayings (*logos*), he shall never taste of death."

" I have given them (the apostles) thy word (*logos*), and the world hath hated them, because they are not of the world, even as I am not of the world."

"The Word (*logos*) was with God, and the Word was God. . . . In him was life; and the life was the light of men."

There is nothing essentially new in this. The word (*logos*), in its lowest stage, is precisely the words (*rêmata*) of life-giving truth in the group above headed "As messenger"; and in idea the consummation is the same, "I and the Father are one." Whatever may be the source of the Prologue, it would appear not to be originally from the pen of the evangelist, who associates the divinity of Christ with his works rather than with his words. In the sixth, seventh, and eighth verses we can even detect what seems to be an interpolation betraying the editorial hand of the evangelist who missed no opportunity to emphasize the preparatory nature of the Bap-

tist's work. Neither would the Prologue appear
to come straight from the author of the speeches.
If we take out the three verses just mentioned,
the rest of the piece displays a directness of composition and a logical concentration quite foreign to the speeches in the Gospel and to the first
epistle attributed to John. And further, though
the thought of the Prologue can be grouped
with verses from the speeches, the term *logos* in
this sense occurs very seldom in the body of the
Gospel, where its place is taken by *rêmata,* and
nowhere in the body of the Gospel do we find a
statement in the first person, I am the word,
corresponding to the avowal in the other groups,
"I am the way," etc. On the whole it is a fair
conjecture that the Prologue is the work of
neither the evangelist nor the author of the
Logia, but of some one who perceived clearly
the drift of the Logia, grasped their inmost
spirit, and expressed this in language borrowed
from the philosophical schools of Alexandria.

CHAPTER XI

THE SON OF GOD

OUR study of the fourth Gospel leads, then, to
the conclusion that, apart from the Prologue,
the book falls into two main divisions, one from
some unknown writer, which presents Jesus as
basing his authority on the exercise of supernatural powers, the other, probably from the
Apostle John, which pretends to report the
speeches of Jesus. Of the thaumaturgic Christ
of the evangelist we may say that the picture is
not historical. The Logia raise a more delicate
problem. It may be, it apparently is, a fact that
Jesus never openly uttered such claims as are
attributed to him, and that these speeches place
in his mouth words which really belong to the
reporter. But it is true also, as we have seen,
that these additions of the reporter glide by
almost imperceptible steps from the actual sayings of Jesus to their boldest expansion. At the
least we have in the direct statements of divinity,
such as "I and the Father are one," and "I am

the way, the truth, and the life," the impression
left on the mind of a sympathetic hearer by the
language of his adored Master; we have the
thoughts of a disciple of Jesus, at the end of
long years of brooding on the mystery of that
authority which even from unwilling lips wrung
the confession that "never man spake like this   Jn. vii, 46
man." At the least we have expansion, not
innovation.

It would be much to our purpose if we could
believe unreservedly that these speeches of the
fourth Gospel in their essential conception of
Jesus' self-consciousness go back to the Apostle
John, but the goal we have in view does not depend solely upon such an hypothesis. It is still
a fact, whatever we think of the authorship of
that book, that its higher reaches of theology
might be based upon sayings of Jesus recorded
in the Synoptics, even in Mark. And this fact,
in view of the strong tendency to admit the
general historic authenticity of Mark and of
the so-called Matthean Logia, is of the utmost
importance. It will be remembered that in
our discussion of the ethical and eschatological
teaching of Jesus we designedly left out of account the one point which distinguishes his doctrine from that of the canonical prophets, and

which made of Christianity at once a continuation of the Hebrew religion and a new faith. That point was precisely the personal pretensions of Jesus himself to an authority, not incompatible with, yet of a different order from, his office as Jewish Messiah. In the first chapter of Mark this note is struck unmistakably. Thus we read that a leper came and knelt to him, saying, "If thou wilt, thou canst make me clean." And Jesus, moved with compassion, replied, *"I will,* be thou clean." Who, then, is this that speaks with a personal finality higher than the royal *Le roi le veult?* And in the next chapter the same consciousness of authority is expressed in spiritual matters, when he said to one sick of the palsy, "Son, thy sins be forgiven thee." Who is this that calmly, with a word, presumes to loosen the bonds of sin? The scribes sitting there had no doubt of the meaning of such a command; they reasoned in their hearts: "Why doth this man thus speak blasphemies? who can forgive sins but God only?"[1] Such is the personal note that runs all through Mark, and is—or perhaps I should say, used to be—minimized in the endeavour to draw a sharp line between the

1, 40

11, 5

---

1 According to Dalman, *Die Worte Jesu,* 215, at no time did the Jews ever grant to the Messiah the power of remitting sins.

humanitarian Christ of the Synoptics and the
deified Christ of John. A few other citations
will be sufficient:—

"Verily I say unto you, All sins shall be for- iii, 28
given unto the sons of men, and blasphemies
wherewith soever they shall blaspheme:

"But he that shall blaspheme against the Holy
Ghost hath never forgiveness, but is in danger
of eternal damnation:

"Because they said, He hath an unclean
spirit."

(Clearly, Jesus is laying claim to a special
union with the Holy Spirit, and Matthew, xii,
32, and Luke, xii, 10, quite miss the point when
they add the distinction: "Whosoever speaketh
a word against the Son of man, it shall be forgiven him; but whosoever speaketh against the
Holy Ghost, it shall not be forgiven him.")

"Be of good cheer; it is I; be not afraid." vi, 50
(Compare John xvi, 33.)

"Whosoever will come after me, let him deny viii, 34
himself, and take up his cross, and follow me. . . .

"For what shall it profit a man, if he shall
gain the whole world, and lose his own soul?"

"O faithless generation, how long shall I be ix, 19
with you? how long shall I suffer you? bring
him unto me." (Compare John xiv, 9.)

"Whosoever shall receive one of such children ix, 37
in my name, receiveth me; and whosover shall
receive me, receiveth not me, but him that sent
me."

This last statement, with its negative "receiveth not me," brings us to certain passages that have always been stumbling blocks to the orthodox. To the rich young man who hailed Jesus as "Good Master," he retorted, "Why callest thou me good? there is none good but one, that is, God." Oceans of ink have been spilt to interpret these words so as to mitigate Christ's apparent rejection of divine goodness; yet it might seem that our wonder ought rather to be directed to the extraordinary character of the negation. Consider for a moment what we should think of a man today who, being addressed as good, should solemnly waive the epithet with the denial, "No, only God is good." And so of that other denial which has worried the pedantic exegetes: "Heaven and earth shall pass away, but my words shall not pass away. But of that day and that hour knoweth no man, no, not the angels which are in heaven, neither the Son, but the Father." At an early date the phrase "neither the Son," which limits the omniscience of Jesus, caused offence, and in many manuscripts, including the text accepted by the makers of our Authorized Version, it was omitted from the verse as repeated by Matthew. Yet, taken with what precedes, the words, one thinks,

x, 17

xiii, 31

might pass without troubling the most tender conscience. Again, the implication of the denial is more startling than most of the positive statements of the Gospel; for what should we say to a man who goes out of his way, while setting himself above the angels, to discriminate between himself and God the Father?

So far we have confined our attention to Mark and to passages which are pretty generally recognized as authentic; but the impression they create might be more than confirmed by the other two Synoptics. As the climax of all comes that magnificent chapter of Matthew, the eleventh, beginning with the departure of the twelve disciples on their missionary journey, proceeding to Jesus' reply to the messengers from John the Baptist, passing on to the bitter denunciations of the cities wherein his preaching had been of no avail, and closing with the wonderful "jubilation" and call to the weary and heavy-laden. I have already made use elsewhere[2] of the extraordinary confession wrung from Walter Pater by this summons, but the anecdote is so pertinent to the present theme as to warrant repetition. Mrs. Humphry Ward in her *Recollections* tells how once in Oxford

[2] *Shelburne Essays*, XI, 260.

she was expatiating to Pater on the certain downfall of the orthodox views of Christ under the blows of historical criticism, expecting his assent, and how she was surprised by his answer:

" 'I don't think so,' he said. Then with hesitation: 'And we don't altogether agree. You think it's all plain. But I can't. There are such mysterious things. Take that saying, "Come unto me, all ye that are weary and heavy-laden." How can you explain that? There is a mystery in it—a something supernatural.' "

Now perhaps the first feature of the whole jubilation to strike the mind is the way it falls into the rhythmically balanced structure of ancient prophecy. And this becomes more striking if the passage is printed, as it should be, in verse-lengths:

I thank thee, O Father, Lord of heaven and earth,
Because thou hast hid these things from the wise and
    prudent,
And hast revealed them unto babes.
Even so, Father: for so it seemed good in thy sight.
All things are delivered unto me of my Father:
And no man knoweth the Son, but the Father;
Neither knoweth any man the Father, save the Son,
And he to whomsoever the Son will reveal him.
Come unto me, all ye that labour and are heavy laden,
And I will give you rest.
Take my yoke upon you, and learn of me;

For I am meek and lowly in heart:
And ye shall find rest unto your souls.
For my yoke is easy, and my burden is light.

But the prophetic strain goes beyond the matter of form. The thought and the very language are a close echo of Scripture, and can almost be reconstructed from verses out of the semi-canonical book of Sirach, thus:

I will praise thee, O Lord, King.
Come unto me, ye that desire me,
And fill yourselves with my fruits.
Those that eat of me shall ever hunger,
And those that drink of me shall ever thirst.[3]
Draw near unto me, ye that are uninstructed,
And dwell in the house of instruction.
Submit your neck to my yoke, and let your soul receive
    instruction;
It is near, that ye should find it.
Look upon me with your eyes,
That I have laboured little and have found much rest for
    myself.[4]

The parallel is notable, yet the difference is even more significant: in Sirach the speaker is a per-

_____
[3] The meaning is the same as John's "shall never hunger or thirst," the object understood being reversed.
[4] In place of this last verse the speaker in Matthew probably had in mind a similar clause in Jeremiah vi, 16: "And ye shall find rest for your souls." If so, it is notable that he used the Hebrew text, which reads *margoaʻ*, resting-place $=\dot{\alpha}\nu\dot{\alpha}\pi\alpha\upsilon\sigma\iota\varsigma$, rather than the Septuagint, which wrongly translates $\dot{\alpha}\gamma\nu\iota\sigma\mu\dot{o}\nu$.—The whole passage as quoted is from chapters xxiv and li of Sirach.

sonification of abstract Wisdom, whereas in Matthew the words are put into the mouth of a man, Jesus. The full meaning of this change can be understood by considering other passages of the Old Testament in which Wisdom speaks, and which must have been in the mind of the speaker in the New Testament; for instance these verses in Proverbs:

vii, 22   "The Lord created me in the beginning of his ways, before his works of old.

27   "When he prepared the heavens, I was there: when he set a compass upon the face of the depth.

32   "Now therefore hearken unto me, O ye children; for blessed are they that keep my ways.

35   "For whoso findeth me findeth life."

Now to the sceptical critics the fact that the jubilation in Matthew is a texture of phrases from the Old Testament affords proof sufficient that it is an artificial product of the evangelist and cannot be an authentic utterance of Jesus. I see no force at all in the argument. Perhaps Jesus knew the Scripture as well as did the writer of the Gospel; we have seen indeed how thoroughly his language and ideas were coloured by reminiscence of the prophets, and what could be more natural than that in a moment of su-

preme exaltation he should have fallen into the
full prophetic style? No, the passage, in substance at least, is genuine, the very pith and
marrow of the assumption that runs through the
Synoptics and in the fourth Gospel merges im-
perceptibly into the high theology of the Word.

There it is, the mystery, the something supernatural, the words that never man spake, the
veiled utterance of a pretension that opens the
door to strange speculations. Other leaders of
religious movements have assumed the authority of divine inspiration, but I do not know
where in the books of the world you will find
anything quite equivalent to that "Come unto
me" spoken by an historical man who professed in the same breath to be, and in life showed
himself to be, "meek and lowly in heart." If the
saying is genuine, as we have reason to hold
it, then we must acknowledge that Jesus arrogated to himself something more than belongs
to humanity.

It will have been observed that for the most
part those utterances in Mark and Matthew
show no tinge of that apocalyptic style connected with the office of the Jewish Messiah
which elsewhere dominates the synoptic account,
and that in this respect they are in line with the

fourth Gospel which virtually eliminates the Messianic eschatology from its presentation of Jesus. They are not exactly incompatible with the assumption of the Messiahship, but they pass it by and in a manner transcend it. The eschatology of Mark centres upon the call to repentance in view of an impending event, an event in which certainly Jesus was to play an important rôle as judge and king, but which dominated the imagination by virtue of its own tremendous consequences. Now the appeal is rather to the personal loyalty of the disciples, with no thought, no express mention at least, of the kingdom of heaven, and the person who demands this loyalty bases his right upon no predicted glorification but upon present authority of a spiritual order. He speaks, one might say, not as the Jewish Messiah but as the Saviour of the world. How shall we reconcile these two diverse, if not contradictory, elements in his self-consciousness? What is the relation one to the other?

To the historical critic the outstanding fact connected with the so-called Messianic self-consciousness of Jesus is that he prophesied of himself that which did not come to pass. This to Strauss, who was the first to lay stress on the historic authenticity and the literal sense of the claims of Jesus to be the Messiah, could be explained only in one of two ways: either Jesus did not believe what he was preaching, in which case he was a *Prahler* and *Betrüger,* a lying braggart; or he believed, in which case he was a *Schwärmer,* a fanatical enthusiast. And in this form the dilemma has become classical, generally with the inference, as in Strauss himself, that the latter of the alternatives is correct. So, for instance, Huxley repeats the charge: "If he believed and taught that [*i.e.,* his speedy return], then assuredly he was under an illusion, and he is responsible for that which the mere effluxion of time has demonstrated to be a prodigious error."[5] On this ground to the modern school of psychiatry Jesus was simply a paranoiac.[6]

Naturally such a dilemma, with its possible hideous conclusion, has been a source of anguish to theologians, and naturally they have striven to avoid impalement by slipping round it on one side or the other. The tough-minded sceptic, to change the metaphor, has boldly thrown out the

---

[5] *Essays,* V, 303.
[6] Charles Binet-Sanglé, as the conclusion of his four-volume study of *La Folie de Jésus,* discovers a *Juif, célibataire, dégénéré, aliéné, paranoïaque, mégalomane, théomégalomane hystéroïde.*

child with the bath by denying all historic authenticity to the Gospels whatsoever. That is an honest but a desperate remedy. The liberal theologian, who would retain some reverence for the founder of his religion, effects an escape by declaring that Jesus himself never assumed the rôle of Messiah or made any supernatural claims for himself, but that all such statements were foisted upon him after his death by the community. This, at the least, is disheartening, in that it reduces Christianity to the pale phantom of humanitarianism; it is precarious also, in that it goes so far with the tougher sceptics and thinks it will not have to go further. The more orthodox theologian just shuts his eyes to the issue, or hopes to evade it by softening the offensive kingdom of heaven into subtle allegory of the Church. This, we must say, is foolish or dishonest; it drives the holder to manhandle the texts in a manner which, since the days of Strauss, is really unpardonable.

Such is the problem. We believe that the Messianic utterances of Jesus in the Synoptics are in the main genuine, though as recorded they have undergone certain unessential modifications; we believe that he did veritably acknowledge himself to be the Christ, the Son of the

Blessed, whom the men of his own generation should behold sitting on the right hand of power and coming in the clouds of heaven. He did not so appear, and must be accounted, in some sense of the word, to have suffered under an illusion. Is there any way of taking the sting out of the epithet that German theology has attached to one so deluded—*Schwärmer?*

The Messianic predictions of Jesus were erroneous. Grant that. But take into consideration those other claims to a spiritual authority of a different order, as we read them in Mark. Their authenticity is supported by the soundest historical criticism. Consider, further, that these claims, inevitably veiled when spoken by mortal lips in the towns of Galilee, were developed legitimately by the author of the speeches in the fourth Gospel, whom for convenience' sake we will call John. A sound literary criticism will, I think, concede so much. Then suppose not only that John expresses truly the meaning implicit in the words of Jesus, but that in so speaking Jesus was not deceived about himself. *Suppose that the Son of man was also, in some ineffable manner, the Son of God!*

Oh, the supposition is large. I know that it runs counter to the preconception on which the

fabric of modern Christology is raised. To go
back to the source of all our higher criticism,
Strauss everywhere assumes as self-evident that
anything supernatural cannot be historical. "At
least," he says, "we know certainly what Jesus
was not and did not, viz. nothing superhuman."[7]
Such an assumption really, of course, begs the
question; since the whole issue at stake is just
this, whether Jesus was or was not in some way
superhuman. But Strauss had with him overwhelmingly the critical and scientific tendency
of the age, and he has been followed by virtually
all the liberal theologians from that day to the
present hour. Now I have tried to show, in the
first chapter, that this preconception philosoph-
ically is unjustifiable, that, on the contrary, the
supposition of a higher nature resident within
our human nature is of itself no more irrational
than that operation of mind in body which every
act of existence forces us to accept. But—and
this I have conceded—because the union of the
divine and the human is not to be rejected out
of hand as psychologically impossible, it does
not therefore follow that Jesus of Nazareth was

---

[7] *Leben Jesu*,[4] Works ed. by Zeller, III, 204.—Compare p. 257:
*Ein Jesus, der solche Dinge von sich aussagen kann, ist für die
historische Betrachtung nicht vorhanden.*—The first edition of
the Life appeared in 1835.

actually divine, as he claimed to be. Nor does it fall within the scope of this treatise to attempt to prove the validity of those claims. Such an argument belongs to a work of apologetic and would carry us far beyond our chosen field. The answer to the question must be left to each individual, as he reads the New Testament and reflects on what it means to him and has meant in history. I only ask my reader to suppose the divinity of Christ, and to weigh the consequences.

Evidently, under that supposition, the Messianic problem acquires a new colour. The fact remains that Jesus predicted of himself what did not come to pass; but on the ground of that error we should not simply dismiss him as one of the long list of human fanatics; we should now ask how it happened that he to whom we grant supernatural qualities could have fallen into so serious a mistake in regard to his own mission. How can we marry such ignorance to such a being? In no wise, I think, unless we cling resolutely to the mystery of dualism, and remember that he was human as well as divine, that, in the hard language of the Council of Chalcedon, he was both man and God. I know that the paradox of dualism, however it may be rooted in the ultimate facts of our experience, is repugnant to reason, more repugnant even than the admission of a divine personality. And so it happens that the course of orthodox theology, beginning with Cyril of Alexandria, has inclined to avoid this paradox by minimizing, or eliminating, the humanity of Christ, while emphasizing his divinity. Thus, to take a popular work of the day, written by Dom Anscar Vonier of the Order of Benedictines in England and published with the *imprimatur* of the Roman Church, one meets with such phrases as the "omnipotence of Our Lord's Humanity" and his "infinity of knowledge."[8] And when this infinity of knowledge is confronted with statements like that of his ignorance regarding the day of the kingdom, recourse is had to the so-called economical reserve of Christ which led him, somehow for the salvation of his hearers, to pretend to be ignorant of what he really knew. This concealed monophysitism, to employ the technical term which will become more familiar to us in the next volume of this series, has infected deeply the orthodox theology of the Church both Catholic and Protestant, as could be demonstrated by abundant references, were this the place to do so. But it is contrary to the

[8] *The Personality of Jesus,* 80, 104.

formulation of doctrine which is still held, verbally, as the rock on which Christianity rests. It
makes nonsense of the Gospel record; for surely,
if anything is plain, the Jesus of the New Testament, whatever else he may have been, was one
who lived under the conditions of humanity.
Even John, who writes to exhibit him as the
preëxistent Son of God, portrays him also as a
veritable man. He was weary; he wept; he was
vexed in spirit; he accomplished nothing of himself; he was made flesh. And in the Synoptics
the human side is so emphasized, the limitations
of his knowledge are so manifest, that the problem has been rather to discover his divinity
through the veil of his mortal nature. He "was   Heb. iv, 15
in all points tempted like as we are, yet without
sin." No, the hated paradox of dualism cannot
be avoided; the rationalism of the monophysite
theologian is even less tenable than the rationalism of the humanitarian liberal. The Fathers
at Chalcedon were right.

If you ask how this can be, how the divine and
the human could dwell together without the one
cancelling the other, how knowledge and ignorance can abide in unison, I will say frankly that
I do not understand. Neither do I comprehend
any better how my own body and soul exist to-

gether. But I repeat that, unless we descend to a purely humanitarian view of Christ or lose our hold of reality in a metaphysical theology, we have simply to accept the mysterious fact in the humility of faith. The technical term for this mystery is Kenosis, taken from the great passage in Philippians: "Who, being in the form of God, thought it not robbery to be equal with God, but made himself of no reputation, and took upon him the form of a servant, and was made in the likeness of men." The verb (*ekenôsen*) here translated "made of no reputation" signifies primarily "to make empty (*kenos*)," or, as it came to mean in later Greek, "to make void," "to make of no avail," "to nullify"; and so Kenosis, applied to the preëxistent Son of God, expresses a voluntary invalidating of his divine powers, including knowledge, while yet his lordly prerogative remained intact. In a dim way we can illustrate the meaning of this by comparing the divine "condescension," as it is called, with the act of a mature man who joins a group of children to share in some game of imaginary characters. To do this successfully he gives himself to a voluntary suspension of his intellect; for the occasion he does really take upon himself the child nature, entering into its

ii, 6

emotions and submitting in a measure to its limitations; while all the time he retains a kind of subconsciousness, or consciousness in deliberate abeyance, that he is playing a double rôle. His adult intelligence is still there, asserting itself in various ways, and is capable of asserting itself completely at his volition.

The comparison is inadequate and leaves the Incarnation still an unspoken secret. But even so, one can see that the doctrine of Kenosis throws a new light on the relation of the spiritual claims of Jesus to his Messianic rôle. Suppose he was the divine Son, the Logos, but was only vaguely, perhaps increasingly, aware of this through the veil of his manhood. His consciousness would be coloured by his environment. He would think and speak in the language of the Messianic hope of his people and his age, though, even so, with a profounder grasp of its real import; while occasionally the sense of his universal mission as revealer of God and Saviour of mankind would break through. There was something of this double note in the prophets, who spoke now as though only the Jews were chosen for the kingdom, and now as though all the righteous of the earth were to be gathered in. And from the practical side, judging the case

from our imperfect knowledge of the methods
of Providence, we cannot see how otherwise the
economy of salvation could have been carried
out. It is a commonplace of history that Christianity could have prevailed only when Rome
had made the world one nation. But we do not
reflect also that Christ could have effected his
purpose nowhere else except in Israel, with
its tradition of prophecy. One thinks, perhaps,
of the Greeks, with their keener intelligence,
their philosophical enlightenment, their, in
some respects, profounder perception of spiritual values; but behind their civilization lay the
background of an unredeemed mythology. Philosophy was almost baffled by the hoary tradition of the Greek pantheon; religion could make
nothing of it. It is inconceivable that the new
faith should have been grafted upon the tales of
Zeus. No, the Incarnation in its divine simplicity cannot be imagined outside of Israel, nor in
Israel save at that juncture of history. And the
Incarnate could not have appeared to the Jews
who first accepted him save as their Messiah, nor
could his appeal to repentance have been effective save through the preaching of the immediately expected kingdom. All that is involved

in the self-deception of Jesus; if he was a *Schwärmer,* the word has lost its sting.

In his manner of preaching the kingdom and repentance Jesus went back to the spirit of prophecy which the Jews of his day had slighted for the Law, and to which as a nation they were never able to return. In his appeal, Come unto me, he added to religion that which no prophet had presumed to utter of himself or had even ventured to ascribe to the Messiah. And, reflecting on these things, I ask myself whether for two thousand years men have deceived themselves in believing that in those words they hear a voice summoning them to the peace of God. My imagination staggers in the attempt to reckon what it may have cost to make that cry audible in this thick air to these dull ears and alienated hearts of ours. Is it true that, coming to him, we come to the unseen Father?

CHAPTER XII

MIRACLES AND THE
RESURRECTION

JESUS did not reappear to the men of his generation in the clouds as the glorified judge of the world; did he reappear to his disciples in any manner whatsoever? That is the question raised by the miracle of the Resurrection; but before undertaking to answer it we shall do well to get clear in our mind what we mean by miracle in general.

Now if we take the miraculous to signify merely what is mysterious and inexplicable, all men accept it, must accept it; no one can escape the fatal truth that in whatever direction we push our intellect, we come at last upon the bare fact of something that is there and cannot be explained. Existence itself in this sense would be the ultimate miracle; the strangest of all facts, the most incredible of all facts, which nevertheless all sane men believe, is simply that I am and the world is.

More precisely, however, the miraculous means not merely the mysterious and inexplicable, but that order of the mysterious which offers particular difficulties to our credence for one of two reasons: either, first, because it runs counter to some preconceived theory, or, second, because it is not *forced* upon our belief by contributory evidence. And men are divided correspondingly by their attitude towards the miraculous into two classes: the rationalist and the sceptical, or Platonic, dualist.

The difference lies in this. The rationalist insists on reducing all existence to one order, and further, so far as rationalism takes a scientific turn, on limiting all existence to what can be expressed finally in the mechanical and mathematical terms of physics. He will admit, if he retains his senses, that all things end in mystery, as frankly and willingly as any other man; he knows that his elementary terms, such as mass and energy and motion and number, bring him face to face with naked facts behind which the baffled mind cannot go; but his faith in the regularity of a world-law he has staked on the theory that there is, and can be, no mysterious forces of another order which break into the phenomena of his observation and thwart what he calls the conservation of energy. Anything that runs counter to his preconceived theory of uniformity—for in truth it is a pure preconception of reason, not derived from experience—he classifies as a miracle. Mystery he accepts, perforce; miracle he rejects out of hand.

The sceptical dualist, on the contrary, admits on the basis of what seems to him incontrovertible evidence a division, or discontinuity, in the order of existence, and consequently two realms of mystery which cross each other incalculably and double-bar the gates of ignorance upon the too curious intellect. For him there is no hard and fast line, as the rationalist sees it, between mystery and miracle; he expects, and as a matter of fact finds, a certain reasonableness in the events themselves, but he rejects no order of events by virtue of a preconceived theory of continuous uniform law. In every case he waits upon the evidence.

The bifurcation between the rationalist and the dualist is brought out sharply and fully discussed in the *Phaedo,* where Plato reports Socrates' reasons for breaking with the mechanical monism of Anaxagoras; but for our purpose we may perhaps best reach an understanding of their attitude towards the supposed miracles of the New Testament by starting from the point at which the divergence begins.

Take the simplest act conceivable, the raising of my arm at will. Here the dualist sees the concurrent operation of two radically distinct orders of existence: the material, spatial, mechanical, and the immaterial, non-spatial, mental. He does not pretend to explain how this operation takes place: neither the ultimate mystery of body, nor the ultimate mystery of thought, nor how body affects mind and mind affects body. Now, grant this initial dualism of mind and body, and the facts, or reputed facts, of life follow with no essential increase of mystery, and the only question for him at each step will be: have we or have we not sufficient evidence to *compel* belief. He will of course test the evidence with particular care where the reported event seems in itself to be unreasonable; but, even so, he is open to conviction. Miracle for the dualist begins when the evidence for a particular order of events is doubtful. He does not call the raising of the arm at will a miracle for the simple reason that the evidence of the fact is here so overwhelming as to render denial impossible; familiarity has deadened wonder, if it has not bred contempt.

It is really because of these disturbing sequences that the rationalist takes a stand at the initial point of dualism. That the raising of the arm contains a mystery he will admit, but that it involves the concurrent operation of two radically distinct orders of existence he will obstinately deny. Such concurrence from his point of view would be a miracle, and all miracles he rejects; they are all alike, with no difference in degrees of credibility, all equally impossible on the basis of his preconceived monism. And so he sets to work to devise theories which will explain mind in terms of body, or body in terms of mind, energy in terms of matter or matter in terms of energy—anything to shut tight the door against the first intrusion of dualism—with what extraordinary disregard of facts, what fantastic unreason, and what obscurantism of technical jargon, I have tried to indicate in the introductory chapter of this book.

The next step would be that in which the mind of one man, by the intervention of a perceptible medium, affects another mind and so operates on a body not its own. For instance, I say to a friend, "Come, I have need of you"; and that word "come," spoken or written, affects his mind with emotions that result in corporeal ac-

tivity. Or, a Napoleon pronounces the word
"War," and forthwith millions of minds are influenced and enormous mechanical motions follow. How can this be explained by any known
law of mechanics? There is no relation expressi-
ble in mechanical terms between the energy ex-
erted in pronouncing the word and the changes
in physical motion produced by it; yet the fabric
of science, and the rationalism that goes with
science, rests on Newton's law that any change
in the motion of a body must be caused by the
motion of another body, and that the resultant
motions can be measured in terms of action and
reaction. What has happened in the case proposed? According to his preconceived theory
the rationalist ought to say that this was a miracle and had never happened at all. As a matter
of fact he simply leaves such a case out of his
reckoning. The Platonist sees here not a miracle,
but only a continuation of the mysterious dualism which Socrates maintained against the
Anaxagoreans.

A further step would be the influence of one
mind on another without the intervention of a
perceptible medium, the phenomena commonly
called telepathy. Now intrinsically it is no more
wonderful that A should draw B to him by an

unexpressed volition than through the medium of language. What, after all, is the efficient cause in the sound or sign of COME? The sound or sign is a mere symbol which conveys an idea from mind to mind, and which would have been inoperative except for the idea so conveyed. Thus if I pronounced the word *veni* to one who knew no Latin, no effect would ensue, no change in the field of matter; although in itself the sound *veni* is mechanically equal to the sound "Come." But what is this idea? where is it? how does it accompany the symbol? In some inexplicable manner it exists, associated with a world of mechanical forces, acting upon them, yet totally distinguished from them. The transmission of an idea from mind to mind without a perceptible medium seems stranger, and hence more wonderful, than by the utterance of a sound or the writing of a sign only because it is less familiar. To the dualist telepathy does in this sense introduce a new problem, but as to the fact he will hold his judgement in suspense and wait for the proof. So much evidence is already at hand that telepathy seems to him fairly credible, but not proven; it lies on the border line of miracle, in accordance with his conception of the miraculous as the mysterious which is not forced on his belief by contributory evidençe. The rationalist, so long as he remains consistent, simply rejects telepathy as miracle and hence an impossibility, or else tries to dodge the issue by hinting at some extension of purely mechanical physical forces as yet undiscovered.

Still a further step would be the power of my mind to move an *inanimate* body without contact with my own body, that is, telekinesis. Now this, again, intrinsically is no more incredible than telepathy, or indeed than my power to raise my own arm at will; but the evidence for it is slighter than for telepathy, and it therefore falls more clearly in the realm of miracle. The dualist will meet any report of telekinesis with suspicion; not because such an event is in itself impossible, as the consistent rationalist would hold it to be, but because, so far, he has no contributory evidence to support it.

The dualist is sceptical of miracles; the rationalist denies them on dogmatic grounds.

Now on these principles one can understand the present prevailing, though not entirely logical, attitude of the higher criticism towards the works of Jesus recorded in the New Testament. The rationalist still rejects out of hand as unhistorical everything miraculous, but he has

come to be a little less positive as to the exact
line between the miraculous and the natural,
and to deal leniently, one might say condescend-
ingly, with a large group of stories which the
older critics heard with cynical scorn. Thus, he
is very modest about the acts of healing and all
those events which have to do with the influence
of mind upon body not transcending the limits
of telepathy; larger experience has shaken his
confidence in our knowledge of the extent of
the mysterious interaction between mind and
body, and faith-healing no longer appears quite
so miraculous as it did.

In this whole field the sceptical dualist may
boast, I think, a more open-minded and consistent attitude. Seeing no sharp line between mystery and miracle, he is ready to hold his judgement in suspense, and to measure the credibility
of each reported event on the evidence. Perhaps
it would be nearer the mark to say that his interest turns not so much upon the supernatural
in itself as upon the power of faith which seems
to be involved. He will have been struck by the
constant demand of faith made by Jesus on his
disciples and in his popular ministry. No sentence is more frequent in the Gospels than those
beautiful words—beautiful to our ear in their

English sound—"Thy faith hath made thee whole"; to which is sometimes added the equally comforting phrase, "Go in peace." This would seem to have been the Saviour's regular formula of dismissal after his work of physical healing. It was the prelude to the doctrine of the Church —the Greek Church, that is to say, for in the West the doctrine underwent a hateful transformation—that spiritual salvation was the effect of grace, *charis,* acting as an intermediary between the divine will and the human will. Without that concurrent belief Christ could do little or nothing, as he testified in his home town of Nazareth. He wondered, it is said, at their lack of faith, and so passed from their midst. The experience at Nazareth may have been exceptional in the life of Jesus, but coldness of faith, even among those who were closest to him, never failed to excite a feeling of wonder. When he slept in the ship, and the storm arose, and his disciples waked him, his words were: "Why are ye so fearful? how is it that ye have no faith?" Mk. iv, 40 And when Peter expressed surprise that the fig tree had withered at the curse of Jesus, his reply was: "Have faith in God. For verily I Mk. xi, 22 say unto you, That whosoever shall say unto this mountain, Be thou removed, and be thou

cast into the sea; and shall not doubt in his heart,
but shall believe that those things which he saith
shall come to pass; he shall have whatsoever he
saith." To remove mountains with a word is not
exactly the sort of thing we see happening daily,
and even sympathetic readers of the Bible have
felt constrained to explain the saying of Jesus
as a bit of Oriental exaggeration. Perhaps it is
so; yet, after all, what is there in the words more
than in the equally positive, though less con-
Mk. ix, 23 crete, statement: "All things are possible to him
that believeth"? And why should we suppose
that Jesus did not intend what he said to be taken
literally? Miracle of any sort or degree is merely
an irruption into the realm of mechanical causes
from that unseen otherworld of the mind or
spirit which obeys a law of its own. And if mind
can effect any the least change in the field of
material phenomena, why should we be appalled
at the thought of those greater works of the
spirit? It is a question of faith. Without faith
in its power over the body the mind cannot cause
our arm to rise or our foot to move, as we see in
the impotence of an hypnotic patient. Why then,
by an extension of faith, should not the spirit of
man exercise unlimited control over its yielding
environment?

For my own part, if I may express a personal opinion, the question of miracles in general does not interest me much or strike me as very important. I am willing to pass the matter by. Exception, however, must be made in regard to two reported events of a miraculous kind which concern the nature of Christ himself—the virgin birth and the Resurrection. Of the first of these not much need be said. It is so demonstrably a late intrusion into the life of Jesus, so manifestly legendary in construction, and withal so unessential to the Christian faith, that it has been abandoned by the majority of unprejudiced scholars. Paul makes no mention of the myth anywhere, and in two passages uses words which Gal. iv, 4 Rom. 1, 3 imply a natural birth; yet the miracle would have fitted so well into his eschatological scheme, that silence on his part is almost equivalent to proof that the story was not yet current. Mark also has no mention of it; on the contrary he relates an event which indicates pretty clearly that iii, 31 at the first Mary sought to restrain her son from his ministry. Matthew and Luke, no doubt for the sake of the moral attached, repeat the story from Mark, without noting that it is incompatible with the miraculous birth narrated by them elsewhere. As for the narrative itself, in both cases it contains a genealogy of Joseph which patently had been constructed before the legend arose, and which was designed to corroborate the descent of Jesus from David in the male line. Matthew then concludes his genealogy with words which deprive it of any sense: "And Jacob begat Joseph the husband of Mary, of whom [singular, referring to Mary alone] was born Jesus, who is called Christ"; and Luke, who gives a genealogy in reverse order, makes it ridiculous by an interpolation at the beginning: "Jesus . . . being (as was supposed) the son of Joseph, which was the son of Heli, etc." It is perhaps a matter of less significance that the two genealogies cannot be reconciled one with the other, but the general inconsistencies, even contradictions, of the other details confirm the late origin of the story. No open-minded reader can go through the introductory chapters of Matthew and Luke without feeling their legendary character. The absence in John of any reference to the virgin birth has been explained on the ground that the author thought he saw an incompatibility in what by his time must have been an article of the creed with his theory of the Son of God. If Christ was "conceived by the Holy Ghost," then his divine nature would

i, 16

iii, 23

have had a beginning at the same moment with his human nature, and the eternal preëxistence could scarcely be maintained.

We must give up the virgin birth as a late invention, and this, as a matter of fact, can be done with no detriment to the fundamental doctrine of the Incarnation; the divine nature of Christ is better left simply as a mystery for which no biological explanation is offered.[1] But the Resurrection presents a problem of a totally different sort, both critically and theologically. In the first place, in this unlike the virgin birth, it was certainly a matter of belief in the primitive community. Paul gives a precise account of the appearances of Jesus to himself and to the other disciples; he had persecuted the new sect because of its belief in a Messiah who had been crucified and was supposed to have risen from the dead, and, in view of the date of Paul's conversion, that belief must be carried back to the months immediately following Christ's death. And, in the second place, the effect of the belief, however explained, had been tremendous. It trans-

---

[1] I admit the importance of the virgin birth to what may be called the poetical side of worship, but this can be maintained by recognizing its symbolical value, so long, that is, as we hold to the literal fact of the Incarnation. The scope and significance of the symbolical clauses of the creed cannot, however, be dealt with in this volume.

formed a number of disheartened and scattered adherents suddenly into a band of resolute missionaries who were ready to venture their lives on their faith, and whose conviction was sufficiently powerful to turn the current of history. Something happened; how shall we explain it? Here again we may go back to Strauss, who gave the question its classical form. There are, he observes, three ways of dealing with the matter: (1) the older orthodox view, which accepts literally the Gospel account of the Resurrection, (2) the trance, or resuscitation, theory, (3) the hallucination theory. Strauss himself inclines to the third of these as the most plausible escape from the superhuman, but the second has had many advocates among critics of the rationalistic type.

(1) The literal acceptance of the Gospel narrative. This position is convenient, but difficult to defend. The four accounts present so many inconsistencies, not to say downright contradictions, that one hardly sees how they can go back to a single primitive tradition of actual events. Commentators have made desperate efforts to harmonize the Gospels here, but again, as in the case of the virgin birth, have failed lamentably. And apart from these inconsistencies, the nar-

rative bears the unmistakable stamp of legendary invention. It is, for instance, impossible to
form any clear conception of such a body as
Jesus is represented as wearing, a body which
passes through closed doors yet is palpable
and can eat solid food. The Gospel story of the
risen Christ, beautiful though it may be in some
respects, lowers the spiritual life to a semi-
materialism which has left an unfortunate trail
in religion; it ought to be surrendered as pure
superstition, or, at the least, interpreted symbolically. Happily there are other ways of treat-
ing the Resurrection.

(2) The trance, or resuscitation, theory. According to this Jesus did not die on the cross,
but fell into a comatose state from which he re-
vived, or was resuscitated, and so appeared to
the disciples in the flesh. In support of such a
view attention is called to the fact that, appearing to be dead, he did not suffer the breaking of
bones as happened to the malefactors crucified
with him. Contributory evidence to the possibility of revival is drawn from the story of
Josephus, that on a certain occasion he had
found a number of Jews crucified by the Romans, three of whom, as known to him, had been
begged from Titus; and that one of these under

careful treatment was resuscitated.[2] But, as
Strauss points out, the obstacles in the way of
this explanation render it difficult, if not impossible, of credence. A man who came from the
tomb, broken and enfeebled by his experience
on the cross, with unhealed wounds in his hands
and perhaps in his feet, who dragged out a
wretched existence for a short time and then
passed away by a natural death, could not have
impressed his disciples as their glorified Lord,
and could not have started a sincere belief in the
Resurrection such as history demands. The
trance theory must be rejected as a remnant of
the old rationalistic method which sought a mechanical explanation for all the miraculous
events of the New Testament, and which Strauss
put out of court once for all by his conception
of myth.

(3) The hallucination theory. For the basis
of this we turn from the Gospels to the statement of Paul, which connects his personal experience with the tradition of the church in
Jerusalem as he had heard it probably in those
fifteen days spent with Peter and James the
Lord's brother after his conversion. Every word
of the passage is significant:

2 *Vita*, 75.

"For I delivered unto you first of all that I Cor. xv, 8 which I also received, how that Christ died for our sins according to the scriptures;

"And that he was buried, and that he rose again the third day according to the scriptures:

"And that he was seen of Cephas, then of the twelve:

"After that he was seen of above five hundred brethren at once; of whom the greater part remain unto this present, but some are fallen asleep.

"After that he was seen of James; then of all the apostles.

"And last of all he was seen of me also, as of one born out of due time."

In what manner Paul had seen the Lord we know from the triple account in Acts. It is true that these accounts do not agree perfectly in detail and are therefore open to some suspicion, but in the main they accord with what Paul says of himself in the epistles. He was on the road to Damascus for the purpose of persecuting the Christians there, when suddenly he was struck down by a great light, and heard a voice, and beheld a figure which he took to be the crucified and glorified Jesus. Thus, he says, God "called Gal. 1, 15 me by his grace, to reveal his Son in me." Here, manifestly, was an occurrence of a different order from the scenes recorded in the Resurrec-

tion chapters of the later Gospels. What came
to Paul was not contact with a seemingly material body which could be handled as Thomas
felt the wounds in the palpable hands, and which
partook of food on the shore of the Galilean sea;
it was rather in the nature of what we ordinar-
ily call a vision. And so far as the record indicates—this is the important point—the previous
appearances to Peter and the rest were of the
same sort; nor is there a word anywhere in the
epistles implying that the manifestations to the
other apostles were more realistic, as we might
say, than this vision of Paul's. Reading Paul
alone we should gather that Christ had appeared
to the disciples in the fashion described of Ste-
Acts vii, 55   phen, who "looked up steadfastly into heaven,
and saw the glory of God, and Jesus standing
on the right hand of God," or as Peter said in
Acts ii, 32   his sermon on the day of Pentecost: "This Jesus
hath God raised up, whereof we are all wit-
nesses." If the events happened as we infer from
Paul's account, it is perfectly easy to understand how as time passed the tradition took on
flesh and blood, so to speak, and developed such
stories as we find in the later Gospels. That
would be a work of the mythopoeic imagination
corresponding in character to the creation of

legends connected with the birth. Whereas, on the contrary, it is not easy to understand how the story, if it existed primitively as the Gospels record it, should have left no trace in Paul's writings.

I have referred to the later Gospels, meaning thereby Matthew and Luke and John; for with Mark the case is not quite the same. In the first place Mark represents an earlier tradition, and was written, as most critics now hold, soon after the martyrdom of Peter and Paul. It would then have been addressed to readers who had the words of the apostles fresh in memory, and ought to reproduce the tradition in about the same stage as we find it in the epistles. Now Mark, it will be recalled, relates how the two Marys and Salome brought spices to the grave early on the morning of the third day, how they found the stone rolled away, and within the sepulchre beheld an angel who bade them tell the disciples and Peter to go to Galilee where they should see Christ, and how the women fled from the sepulchre and said nothing to any one, "for they were afraid." With these words the narrative abruptly ends, for the conclusion taken over into our Authorized Version is generally recognized as spurious. What has happened? Did the writer, interrupted by death or otherwise, leave his work unfinished, or was the manuscript mutilated at an early date? Both hypotheses are extremely unlikely, the first, considering the little that remained to be written, utterly incredible. Or, as Eduard Meyer suggests,[3] did he purposely leave off here, through awe of a mystery which, as in the case of the temptation, he would hint at without revealing? However that may be, and however we may deplore the loss of what no doubt would have been a more sober tale than that which has come to us in the later books, so much we may conjecture by comparing Mark with Paul. The appearance occurred first on the third day after the burial (reckoning, that is, in the classical style; we should say on the second day after). This is stated definitely by Paul and can be inferred from Mark; it is confirmed by the early consecration of Sunday as the Lord's day. The revelation, the first at least, probably took place in Galilee, whither the disciples fled in dismay after the fatal catastrophe, and not in Jerusalem as Luke and John relate. As for the curious statement of Mark that the women told no one—which is flatly contradicted by the other three evangelists, with the addition in

[3] *Ursprung und Anfänge des Christentums*, I, 18.

Matthew and John that they themselves, or Mary Magdalene alone, beheld the Lord—this would seem to intimate that the story of the women and the empty tomb grew up somehow independently of the major tradition of the appearance to the disciples and only afterwards was connected with that tradition. One can detect in the language of Matthew just how the jointure occurred: "And they departed quickly from the sepulchre with fear *and great joy;* and did run to bring his disciples word." The inhibitive fear of Mark is adroitly translated into the awe of joy.

With this critical study of the sources the theory of hallucination fits in admirably. Nothing really happened, nothing objective that is to say; but Peter and then after him various groups of excited fanatics merely imagined they beheld the risen Lord in glory and heard voices. The objections to the literal and trance theories seem to be obviated, and the whole matter of the Resurrection falls into the comfortable realm of myth; it is just another ghost story.

So it seems—until we reflect. Then we begin to ask whether the explanation is quite so simple as it sounds. Does hallucination work in this way, and can we find any parallel for it in history? We could comprehend the case if Peter alone, or Peter with one or two others, were concerned; but how explain the unanimity of belief among a fairly large company of men? The disciples were scattered and dejected. They might have been called together by Peter, and might have been impressed by the assurance of his vision; but could the apostles at different times and an assembly roughly estimated at five hundred—could they have been hypnotized into believing that they had actually seen the Lord, into believing this so strongly that their faith was suddenly made invincible against the world? It is hard to comprehend. And why should their visions, if due merely to mental excitement, have occurred all within a brief period—forty days, the witnesses said, thinking perhaps of the mystic associations of the number—and then have ceased until the single repetition came to Paul? Why that flurried fanaticism and then complete sobriety? "Such intemperance could never have begotten such temperance."[4] The theory of subjective hallucination is pretty, but when closely examined incredible.

[4] *The Fair Haven*, by Samuel Butler, author of *Erewhon*. One hesitates to cite this sarcastic and ambiguous wit, remembering the caution against *Danaos et dona ferentes*, but I know of no more subtle analysis of Strauss's theory than in this strangely fascinating book.

All the current views fail us; yet there the fact of the belief in the Resurrection remains, still to be accounted for. Now suppose that we accept the critical interpretation of the documents; admit that the Gospel narratives are a tissue of myth, and that for a true conception of the facts we must confine ourselves to Paul. Grant the subjective nature of the events, in the sense that no material palpable body appeared to the disciples. But suppose also that Christ did veritably rise from the grave, that, whatever became of his fleshly tabernacle and however we explain the story of the empty tomb, his spirit lived and went to God. Suppose, if you will, that the Straussian presumption, which rejects anything supernatural as unhistoric, is not the whole truth. Then, I think, that unpleasant word hallucination loses its sting, as did the epithet *Schwärmer*. The appearances of Christ may be regarded as subjective, but not necessarily therefore as vain and illusory dreams. They would have been genuine manifestations of spirit to spirit, the warranty of knowledge, based on miraculous intervention, that he whom they mourned as dead was living with God, their Saviour and victorious King, the dispenser of the Holy Ghost. So, the

Resurrection would be the supreme act of grace, the divine confirmation of our faith in the other-world as an ever-present reality behind these veiling clouds of phenomena; without it the Incarnation would be left a tale of sound and madness, signifying nothing. I see not why the critic imbued with the profounder Platonic scepticism may not reasonably substitute for Strauss's hallucination the comforting phrase of St. Paul, "visions and revelations of the Lord."

II Cor. xii, 1

CHAPTER XIII

CONCLUSION

HOWEVER we interpret the personal claims attributed to Jesus, and whatever construction we put on the story of the Resurrection, one indisputable fact remains, that Christianity began with the belief in a superhuman founder. To the band of apostles and disciples gathered together in Jerusalem after the crucifixion, this Jesus whom they had accompanied in his mission through the lake towns and among the hills of Galilee, a friend quick to respond to all the compassions of humanity yet unyielding in principle and capable at times of scorching indignation, a teacher who arrogated to himself a sublime authority and whose words, marvellously simple and direct, seemed yet to elude them with mysterious hints of a new faith,—to these Christians, as they were soon to be named, their Master appeared in memory to have been a man like to themselves and at the same time something more than man. Now at least, after his humiliation, he had been raised up to stand at the right hand of God as judge and Lord of the world; and in recollection they saw the light of that deification upon his face while he walked with them on the earth. He was the Jesus whom they had known, one person, whether in the flesh or in glory; but his nature presented itself to them in a double aspect, human and divine. This was not a metaphysical theorem, not a doctrine which they had reasoned out, but a conviction born of experience.

At first his divine nature took for them, as Jews, the eschatological form with which they were familiar. Their Lord was the Messiah, the Christ, who should return after no long delay with the hosts of heaven to establish the kingdom of God. And this idea was not the product of their own imagination, but had been held by Jesus of himself and imparted to them in the last days of his life. This eschatological conception was retained by Paul, even in some respects hardened by him, though we are apt to overlook the fact when we read his epistles today. Certainly Paul did not create Christianity or any fundamental belief of Christianity. Something he added, no doubt, from the treasure of his brooding mind. He enlarged what may be called

the cosmic aspect of religion, by his profounder
sense of the eternal design of Providence and
by his corresponding emphasis on the notion of
a preëxistent Christ. Whether his own or not,
the words in Ephesians spring from his inspiration:

"The fellowship of the mystery, which from III, 9
the beginning of the world hath been hid in God,
who created all things by Jesus Christ:

"To the intent that now unto the principalities and powers in heavenly places might be
known by the church the manifold wisdom of
God,

"According to the eternal purpose which he
purposed in Christ Jesus our Lord."

With this expansion of religion went a deep-
ening of the individual note; the soul of man,
with its hopes and fears, its sense of sin and
longing for salvation, was caught up into a celestial drama, and its fate grew to vast significance. The intensity of the personal faith of
Paul became a permanent possession of the
Church to the great enrichment of devotion.
Yet even here one must make reservations; for
much of the bigotry, the emotional mysticism
and spasmodic hysteria that have troubled the
Church from the beginning can be traced to
Paul's insistence on his own miraculous conver-

sion. And upon the foundation of his faith Paul raised a structure of rabbinical theology the harmful effects of which can scarcely be overestimated. His doctrine of predestination and grace, faith and law, went under for a season, and never again won a firm hold upon the Greek community; but in the Occident it reappeared with Tertullian and Augustine, struggled with opposing ideas through the scholastic debates of the Middle Ages, and then burst out with devastating malignity in the theology of Luther and Calvin. The legalistic elements in Paul were naturally sympathetic to the Latin temper, and to them we owe what I must regard as the unfortunate trend taken by Christianity in the Western world.

The unchecked triumph of the Pauline system would have riveted on religion a Jewish Messiah. The current in that direction was diverted by a new spiritual force which, apparently entering the Church through the Hellenistic communities of Asia Minor, reached its climax in the Gospel composed at Ephesus and attributed to St. John. Here indeed the cosmic scope of salvation, which had loomed so large in the imagination of Paul, is continued, but assumes a different colour. Jesus, still the preexistent Son of God, appears no longer as the Hebrew Christ, but as the personified Logos of Greek philosophy grafted upon the Wisdom of the late Jewish thinkers, themselves already half Hellenized; while the kingdom of Jehovah dissolves into the ubiquitous presence of the otherworld. For the rabbinic theology which Paul so to speak had turned against itself, we now have a refined and spiritualized gnosticism. In this scheme the Incarnation becomes not so much a moment in the eschatological drama as the focussing point of God's continuous manifestation of Himself to the human soul; and attention is centred less upon the death than upon the life of the Saviour: "he alone was able to bring light to the souls of men, so that with our own eyes we might discern the way of eternal salvation."[1]

The change was not complete. The ethics of John retain the tone of the Synoptics and of Paul; and the gnosticism of John demands as the central act of faith a conversion of the whole man rather than a mere enlightenment of the intellect. Religion has by no means been swallowed up in metaphysics, nor has the inspiration of prophecy faded into the thin air of specula-

[1] *Clem. Hom.*, i, 19.

tion. And even so the alteration needed in some
respects to be modified or revoked. Thus, for
instance, the peculiar doctrine of the Logos
which prevailed for some time in the East,
proved to contain certain dangerous implications, and during the course of the third century fell into the background of theology. But
in the main Christianity passed with the fourth
Gospel into the wide stream of Greek thought,
while bringing to that Tradition its own vital
contribution; henceforth we have to study the
mutual assimilation of the faith of Jesus with
the Idealism of Plato.

Was this diversion of Christianity a betrayal
of Christ? In answering this question we may
first of all eliminate the objections of those who
would strip religion of its supernatural philosophy altogether, and would reduce it to mere
morality tinctured with trust in the fatherhood
of a tenderly indulgent God. The Jesus of the
humanitarians is a pure fiction, with no warrant
in history. Here there would be no choice between Paul and John; both are equally repugnant to the views of modern liberalism. But what
of Paul's special theology? Certainly, in so far
as John threw over the burden of inverted rabbinic legalism, there was no betrayal; Jesus him-

self in his attitude towards the Law stood rather
with John than with Paul. The question grows
acute only when we consider John's substitution of the Greek revealer of God for the Jewish
Messiah, for here undoubtedly Paul, however
he may have developed the idea, was faithful to
the more literal conception of Christ's mission
held by the primitive Church.

Now we must admit, as in fact I have admitted, that Christianity, as a religion of com-
pelling power, could have taken its origin only
in Palestine, and only through the preaching of
the imminent Messianic kingdom. Greece, with
all her wisdom, could never have given this impulse to the world, and the efforts of Greek philosophy to satisfy the craving for salvation had
failed. But it is also true that the Messianic kingdom, valuable as it was and always may be symbolically, in the larger light of history fades to
a temporary expedient; and the hard fact soon
forced itself upon attention that the Messiah
did not appear, at least in any such realistic fashion as he had prophesied. Christianity to become
a world religion had to be translated into the
universal and more spiritual terms of Greek
intuition. And this, call it the work of Providence or what you will, is what actually hap-

pened. As I see the matter, such a change involved no disloyalty to the author of Christianity, but was a legitimate development of that which lay in the background of his teaching. So far as Jesus' consciousness of his divine nature transcended the limits of Messianism it was already implicitly Greek and not Hebrew. It remained for John, or whomever we call the source of the Logia in the fourth Gospel, under the influence of Hellenistic philosophy to lay hold of those sayings of Jesus which expressed his relation to the Father in general language, and so to fulfil the hidden purpose of the Master, hidden partly perhaps even to himself. Thus only could the accomplishment of prophecy become the universal revelation of God to man. Shall we deem this a betrayal?

Danger there was, as there must be in all reaching after spiritual truth. At an early date the thought of Christ's divinity so enthralled the Greek mind that it threatened to overshadow completely his humanity; and the first great heresy to trouble the Church—and never to be driven out—was the docetism, so-called, which held that Jesus was in no true sense a man at all, but only seemed to be such. Hence the writer of the first epistle of John opens with an earnest insistence on "that which was from the beginning, which we have heard, which we have seen with our eyes, which we have looked upon, and our hands have handled, of the Word of life." In its concern with the revelation of God *to* man the Orient too often forgot the revelation of God *in* man. But withal Greek theology, in its central course and during the period of our study, remained faithful to its origin. For three centuries and a half it wrestled with a succession of heresies which, on one side or the other, sought to rationalize, and in rationalizing virtually to explain away, the mystery of the Incarnation. As a result of that conflict it laid down the one essential dogma of the universal Church, western and eastern, protestant and catholic, the Faith as it was proclaimed at Nicea[2] and at Chalcedon was defined in a series of clauses clear, hard, unargued, unreasoned, impregnable against every possible perversion. That was the virtue of the Greek intelligence, to perceive that beside this dogma all other questions are of secondary importance. And thus it happens today that a churchman may deal with

---

[2] Here again I must remind the reader that the Faith of Nicea is not to be confused with the so-called Nicene creed, which contains matter extraneous to the simple dogma promulgated at the first ecumenical Council. The Faith does indeed demand belief in the Holy Ghost, but not necessarily in a personified Holy Ghost.

the various "creeds" as he will, interpreting
them literally or symbolically to his taste, even
to the point of rejecting the personification of
the Holy Ghost and the consequent doctrine of
the Trinity, whereas, so long as he calls himself
a Christian, he ought honestly and unevasively
and *ex animo* to subscribe to the Faith as finally
formulated at the fourth general Council. The
language of the formula may be repellent to
modern ears, we may perhaps regret that the
exigencies of the long contest with heresy com-
pelled the Fathers to adopt a bolder terminol-
ogy than our understanding of the mystery
warrants; but at bottom the test of orthodoxy
as ultimately defined in the year 451 is no more
than an explicit statement of the faith held so
unequivocally by the little band of disciples at
the beginning, that Jesus of Nazareth, whom
they had known and heard, who had been crucified and, as they believed, had risen from the
dead, was one person of two natures, human and
divine. That is all, and it is enough.[3]

As I have said before, it does not fall within
my design to debate the truth or error of Chris-

---

[3] The Definition of Chalcedon contains a reference to the Virgin
Mary as *theotokos*, or mother of God. But this dubious addition to the Faith is after all introduced only as a confirmation
of the central dogma of the Incarnation and is not essential to
that dogma.

tianity. I have argued that the dualism of faith
cannot on any sound philosophical basis be rejected out of hand as incredible because it is incomprehensible. I have tried to show that the
belief of the Church corresponds with the deeper
self-consciousness of Jesus himself; that is a
problem of historic evidence. But as for the
simple fact, whether Jesus was deceived or not
in his claims, that is a question of a different
sort, to be answered individually by each man
as the voice of conscience responds to the words
spoken so many ages since by the lake of Galilee. Only, thus much I would urge: if the supposition of Christianity be not true, then we
have no sure hope of religion. The Ideal philosophy of Plato waits for its verification upon
no belief in anything outside of what we can
test and know in our immediate experience, and
he to whom the otherworld of Ideas is a reality
possesses a spiritual comfort beyond which it
may be presumptuous to search—I do not say.
But the full scope of religion requires a theology and a mythology as well as a philosophy,
and if the crowning element of religion is to
be more than a reasonable conjecture, as ultimately it was to Plato, if it is to be confirmed by
the certainty of revelation, then I see not whither

we are to turn save to Christianity. For mythology, the crown of religion, is just the coming
together of the human and the divine, the descent
of God to man and the consequent elevation of
man to God. In this sense all religions have their
myths, and might be regarded as the groping of
Acts xvii, 27   men in the darkness, "if haply they might feel
after him, and find him, though he be not far from
every one of us." Even the Buddhist, who in his
dread of metaphysical entities thinks to do without a supreme deity, yet consoles himself with
a variegated history of the Buddha's previous
existences and with naïve tales of a humanized
pantheon.

In contrast with all other religions the peculiar strength of Christianity is that in the Incarnation it reduces mythology to the simplest
possible terms; every extravagance, every overgrowth of fancy, is swept away for the bare fact
that God in Jesus appeared among men. Indeed, of all arguments for the supernatural
origin of the Christian faith the most convincing
is a frank comparison of its superb simplicity
with the wild tumult of Hellenistic supersti-
tions through which it cut its way by what has
the semblance of providential direction. Read
the fragments of literature left to us by the

Orphic and Phrygian and Egyptian and Chaldean mythologies of the age, consider the monstrosities of Mithra and the fabulous follies of Gnosticism, each in its own fashion seeking like Christianity to bridge the gulf between the human and the divine,—and then turn to the Gospel of Mark! It is like coming out into the clear light of the sun from a misty region haunted by

> The ghosts of words, and dusty dreams,
> Old memories, faiths infirm and dead.[4]

To say that the dogma of Christianity is endangered by the comparative study of religions implies a gross ignorance of facts or a wilful misapprehension of values. If there be any true myth, if the divine nature has at any time in any wise directly revealed itself to man, if any voice shall ever reach us out of the infinite circle of silence, where else shall we look but to the words of the gospel? Not Christianity alone is at stake in our acceptance or rejection of the Incarnation, but religion itself.

That is an alternative the modern man does not willingly face, and the desperate endeavour of liberal criticism, so far as it retains the spirit of reverence, has been to evade the issue. In the

[4] Swinburne, *Félise*. Aptly chosen by Mr. Legge as the motto for his *Forerunners and Rivals of Christianity*.

main the attempt has taken the form of an Hegelian substitution of ideals for Ideas, of what we should like to be true for what we believe actually to be true; the value of Christianity shall not be reckoned on the basis of objective truth, on the answer to the question, that is to say, whether Jesus and his disciples were deluded or not, but on the character of their delusion, whether it be beneficent or not. Such was the turn given to apologetics by Strauss; and Schweitzer, summing up the trend of nineteenth-century theology, will say that "in the end it makes no difference to what degree the Incarnation was realized in the person of Jesus, since the idea [rather, the ideal] is a living thing in the community; . . . religion in its essence is independent of any historic fact."[5] Such is the famous philosophy of "modernism," the doctrine that we need not believe but must act as if we believed,—very ingenious, very pretty, but impracticable, and at heart a lie which the world will not tolerate: men will not long act as if they believed. The alternative is the Faith of the Greek tradition or no religion of Christ.

[5] *Geschichte der Leben-Jesu-Forschung*, 81, 519.

THE END